D0773711

Richard Terry Smith 1933-
Fern Marlene Johnson 1935-

FIRES
of
FAITH

Terry's Lineage From Rev. John Rogers (pg 46)

1. Richard Terry Smith   (1933-
2. Bertie Daniels   (1905-1989)
3. Orson A. Daniels.   (1865-1955)
4. Jane Ann Sheffield   (1833-1906)
5. Marie How Mott   (1808-1886)
6. Elizabeth Dwight   (1790-1865)
7. Joseph Dwight Jr.   (1770-1860)
8. Israel Dwight   (1744-1826)
9. Mary Pinchon   (1706-1751)
10. Margaret Hubbard   (1647-1716)
11. Margaret Rogers   (1628-1716)
12. Nathaniel Rogers   (1598-1655)
13. John Rogers   (1571-1636)
14. John Rogers   (1538-1601)
15. Rev. John Rogers   (1507-1555)

Cover art from left to right: *Gutenburg Printing*, courtesy of FIRES OF FAITH; Groberg Films and BYU Broadcasting, Steve Porter photographer. *King Henry VIII*, courtesy Bridgeman Art. *Martyrdom of William Tyndale*, courtesy of FIRES OF FAITH; Groberg Films and BYU Broadcasting, Steve Porter photographer. *John Wycliffe*, courtesy Bridgeman Art. *John Calvin*, courtesy Wikimedia Commons. *An Original King James Bible*, courtesy Harold B. Lee Library, Special Collections, Brigham Young University; *Mary*, courtesy Wikimedia Commons. *Martin Luther*, courtesy Porter Gallery Images.

Interior imagery: All movie stills courtesy of FIRES OF FAITH; Groberg Films and BYU Broadcasting, Steve Porter photographer. Other imagery referenced below each image.

Cover design copyright © 2012 by Covenant Communications, Inc.
Cover and book design by Jennie Williams.

Published by Covenant Communications, Inc.
American Fork, Utah

Printed in China
First Printing: August 2012

19 18 17 16 15 14 13 12   10 9 8 7 6 5 4 3 2 1

ISBN-13: 978-1-60861-905-4

FIRES of FAITH

The Inspiring Story Behind the King James Bible

Written by Brock Brower

with Lee Groberg & Steven Porter

Covenant Communications, Inc.

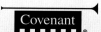

chapter

1

A NEW TRANSLATION

*"If it pleases your majesty, may a new translation be made
That will answer to the intent of the original."*

n 1603, two kingdoms joined together on what Shakespeare gazetted as "this sceptered isle, this precious stone set in a silver sea" to bring forth at long last the United Kingdom of Great Britain. This happened—peacefully, for a change—because one king wielded both scepters. James VI had long been King of Scotland, almost since his birth as the son of Mary Stuart, Queen of Scots, and Lord Henry Stuart Darnley. But she had later abdicated—had been deposed, really, when James VI was not yet two—on suspicion of murdering Lord Darnley and had to flee to England in 1584. On March 22, 1603, the "Virgin" Queen Elizabeth, who had first imprisoned and then beheaded Mary Queen of Scots in 1587 for her treasonous activities, at last lay dying herself at Hampton Court Palace. She summoned her Privy Council to settle the much-disputed question of royal succession.

"Who but our cousin in Scotland?" she ruled imperiously. "I pray you trouble me no more."

Her death the next day ended the powerful rule of the House of Tudor through the entire sixteenth century and brought James VI to London to

At King James's Hampton Court Conference, John Rainolds was the most prominent representative of the Puritan party. He died in 1607 before the KJV Bible was completed. Courtesy Wikimedia.

reign over "England, France, Scotland, and Ireland" as James I of the newly rising House of Stuart.

James was still a young monarch at thirty-six and largely unfamiliar to his English subjects, so they were much concerned over his religious beliefs, which had caused such turmoil during the Reformation under the Tudors. Henry VIII, who was Queen Elizabeth's father, had in 1531 split off the English church from the control of the pope over his controversial divorce from Catherine of Aragon so he could marry Anne Boleyn, Queen Elizabeth's mother. Reigning almost four decades (1509–1547), Henry VIII continued his tumultuous marital life through six different wives in his ever-dynastic hope of fathering a male heir. That tumult was summarized in this folkloric mnemonic: "Divorced (Catherine of Aragon, mother of Queen Mary), beheaded (Anne Boleyn, for adultery), died (Jane Seymour, mother of Edward VI), divorced (Anne of Cleves), beheaded (Katheryn Howard, again for adultery), survived (Katherine Parr)."

To abet these serial marriages, Henry VIII, as monarch, had placed himself at the head of the Church of England, though he always claimed that he and his bishops were never heretics. His daughter, the Good Queen

Mary, Queen of Scots and Almost of England

Mary was only six days old when her royal father died in 1452; nine months later, she was crowned Queen of Scotland. Over her passionate lifetime, she was always the looming Stewart—and Catholic—rival of Elizabeth for the English throne. The first challenge occurred when, at age sixteen, she married a sickly French prince, who became Francis I; Mary was now the future Queen of France. Impoliticly, her French king died one year later, and Mary returned home to marry her cousin Henry Stuart, Lord Darnley, who sired her only child, James. Palace intrigue, largely religious, led to their estrangement. Mary, opposed to any divorce, is believed to have plotted against her own husband. Henry Stuart was found strangled after a mysterious explosion in their own household. Mary next married the Earl of Bothwell, the very Scot who had supplied the gunpowder.

Mary, Queen of Scots, after Nicholas Hilliard, courtesy Wikimedia.

Such intrigue and violence proved too much for the dour Scots. Queen Mary was forced to abdicate in 1567 and later fled to London for protection under Queen Elizabeth. But she continued to hatch plots over the next seventeen years and was eventually tried for treason. On the night before her execution in 1587, she had a remarkable religious confrontation when she swore on a Rheims New Testament to her innocence of any crimes. But the Earl of Kent ruled her oath invalid since it was sworn on a Catholic Bible. "If I swear on the book which I believe to be the true version," answered Mary, "will your lordship not believe my oath more than if I were to swear on a translation in which I do not believe?" But there was no bridging the impasse. She refused the Protestant services of the dean of Peterborough, crossed herself, asked for a Catholic priest to hear her confession, and was again refused. On the morrow, her head was struck off. Over the ensuing years, the party who bore the most unspoken disgrace over the entire bloodletting was her son, James, who remained far too silent about his mother's execution. James was already into his twenties when his mother was beheaded on Queen Elizabeth's hesitant order.

Bess, worked diligently toward the "Elizabethan Settlement" of the newly ordered Church of England along these Anglican lines and against the Jesuitical "priest craft" of the counter-Reformation. But what would now be James's orientation toward religious toleration and issues of church and state? Didn't he come from Scotland, where the chapel was more common than the church? Hadn't he been raised as an abandoned child under the strict Presbyterian doctrines of John Calvin, so might he favor the larger protestant dissent of Martin Luther and his Reformation throughout Europe?

James Stuart did appear a good Christian, with some repute as a biblical scholar. As a young Scottish monarch, he had once tried to launch a translation of the Bible and had himself done metrical translations of thirty psalms, though they were more indicative of his faith than any courtly talent. He also had

King Henry VIII, 1491–1547, ruled from age eighteen until his death. Portrait by Hans Holbein the Younger. Courtesy of Bridgeman Fine Art Library.

a godly fear of witchcraft—every well-informed Christian believed in witches during the seventeenth century—and he had condemned several reputed witches to be burned at the stake. During one prosecution, he had interrogated the witch himself. Shakespeare was aware of this royal interest in sorcery, and he put those three witches into his politic scripting of *Macbeth* in 1607. The tragedy was considered greatly enhanced by the dissembling Weird Sisters, who cleverly predict Macbeth's evil downfall in favor of Malcolm's Scottish lineage of future kings—all, of course, from the House of Stuart. James I, formerly VI, most assuredly was a believer, but might he be one among another growing strain of religious nonconformity—a Puritan?

On his royal procession south, elegantly attended during his six weeks' journey from Edinburgh to London, James was cognizant of his new subjects' agitation over such questions. He realized that Scotch Presbyterianism varied in many practices and preachments from the broader liturgy and richer vestments of the Anglican Church established by the Tudors, especially Henry VIII and Good Queen Bess. And he had

"When James becomes king, he is quickly put in receipt of something called the Millenary Petition. They were from the Puritan wing of the Church and they wanted a simplification of the Church. They were against the whole super-structure of bishops and deans and all the rest of it. Things like vestments and regalia and Catholic idolatrous objects. They wanted simplicity and purity."

—Lucy Worsley
Chief Curator; Historic Royal Palaces, London, England

already been confronted with the so-called "Millenary Petition" from a host of Puritan signatories who sought reforms.

Clearly, trouble lay ahead. So that January after his coronation, James called for a two-day conference among the senior clergy to promote the stability of the Church of England under his new Jacobean dispensation. King James would himself preside over the conference at palatial Hampton Court.

The attending lords of the church, led by the archbishop of Canterbury and the bishop of London, Richard Bancroft, then "stacked" the conference in favor of their own officiating clergy. Seven other bishops, seven deans, and two doctors were added, which meant twenty in all against only four Puritan clerics to be invited. James confidently declared that those assembled "shall change the Church of England. Not only do we want to clarify a number of Church teachings, but it is time to seek new interpretations of the Holy Scriptures." But of some forty proposals for change, not one was approved by the conference nor shown any significant favor by the King himself. James I seemed as set upon his own divine right to rule over the Church of England as he had been when trying to dominate his own Scottish clergy. Some Puritans were already planning a move to Holland, if not yet aboard the *Mayflower*.

At the very close of the conference, during the last minutes of the final afternoon, Dr. John Rainolds, Puritan president of Corpus Christi College, Oxford, arose. "May your majesty be pleased," he shouted repeatedly. "If it pleases your Majesty . . . may a new translation be made that will answer to the intent of the original."

At that juncture, Bishop Bancroft quickly leapt to his feet and declared, according to the record, "my lord of London well added, that if every man's humour should be followed, there would be no end of translating." The archbishop knew Dr. Rainolds favored the Protestant translation known then as the Geneva Bible for its origins from across the English Channel as an imported, sectarian, oft-condemned but fast-selling English version of God's Word, and this was his chance to champion the extant English version named for his own bishopric's closely watched interests—the Bishops' Bible. There was supposed to be one in every church, even though by 1604 the more popular Geneva Bible had gone through ninety-two editions—entire editions, not just so many printings, of what had once amounted to religious contraband, often thrown by church officials on the burn pile. The Geneva Bible was not at all any favorite of James Stuart either, since the unwelcome marginal notes were sometimes critical of royal power: Herod was "a bad king" for having ordered, of all things, the Slaughter of the Innocents.

King James I of Scotland invited both Puritan and Protestant leaders to gather recommendations as to how to best meet the religious needs of his subjects.

But the King himself chose to speak out, if hesitantly, again according to the record: "Whereupon his Highness wished that some special pains be taken in that behalf for one uniform translation (professing that he could never yet see a Bible well translated in English; but the worst of all"—he took pains to add—"his Majesty thought the Geneva to be). . . ." The King allowed that his lapse, this unorthodox glance through a Geneva, chanced to have been into one "given him by an English lady." But the record shows that, at age thirteen, James had been presented—dedicated

Several Bibles, including the Geneva Bible, the Great Bible, the Matthew Bible, and the Bishops' Bibles. Courtesy of Joe and Jeanne Groberg Collection, on loan to Special Collections, Brigham Young University–Idaho Library. Kimball Ungerman, photographer.

to him as "the richt excellent richt high and michtie prince James the Sext King of Scottis"—the first Bible printed in Scotland, the Bassadyne Bible (Edinburgh, 1579), which was indeed a Geneva version.

Obviously His Majesty was prepared to take the risk created by the troublesome Puritans to fuss over yet another revamp/rewrite of the Holy Bible. Such might keep everybody sufficiently occupied to avoid denominational mischief. So during the tense closing moments of the Hampton conference, "yet hereupon did his Majesty begin to bethink himself of the good that might ensue by a new translation, and presently after gave order for this translation which is now presented unto thee."

Thus did these clarion words from the bishopric's engrossing preface introduce the King James Version, today often labeled the KJV, to the English reader seven years later in 1611, launching a Bible that still stands four centuries later as the best-selling book the world has ever known.

The Catholic Church translated the Bible into English at the Rheims monastery. Named the Douay-Rheims Bible, it allowed the church members to also hear the words of the Bible in a more common tongue.

chapter

2

GOD'S WORD

Here we must pause to ask what we are truly dealing with in any Bible that constitutes the Word of God. "In the beginning was the Word," begins the Gospel of St. John, "and the Word was with God, and the Word was God." Still, where exactly does that leave the "original" words—and the plural is all-important here as an indicator of a living, entirely human language—upon which "the intent" of any "new translation" must always be based?

In other words—again plural—we are concerned here with what followed from any revelation of the Word . . . after the Word was somehow presumably spoken.

We have already gotten far beyond *vox clamantis in deserto*—"a voice crying in the wilderness," from John the Baptist—or any Burning Bush, or even commandments scratched with a sculpting fingernail upon stone tablets as an angry Jehovah dictated, and are looking instead toward the holy scriptures copied and illuminated in many a monkish hand or even the Dead Sea Scrolls, reaffirming as late as 1956 the correct attribution of the sacred Word after more than three millennia of contentious debate. In the beginning there was the Word, but only the Word, and the Word was at best an oral tradition. The Word was only limited parole evidence, as it is so often defined in the courts of law—hearsay, if you will—later recorded as holy scripture to vouchsafe

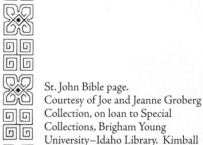

St. John Bible page.
Courtesy of Joe and Jeanne Groberg
Collection, on loan to Special
Collections, Brigham Young
University–Idaho Library. Kimball
Ungerman, photographer.

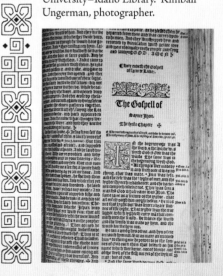

what was comprehended by inspired scribes who sought to transcribe God's holy Word.

Yet again, there remains the uncertain provenance of even these hallowed documents, since no original book attesting to the actual Word of God from either the Old or New Testament exists today. No notes were taken by Job's visitors; no letters from Paul survive. The first Hebrew scrolls were lost with the vanished Ark of the Covenant during the Babylonian Captivity, the tongue itself forgotten and acknowledged dead. We have only later copies, many in other tongues ranging from Hebrew to Greek to Latin and everything in between. When, we must ask, did the Tetragrammaton (YHVH, or Elohim) recall His unknowable name and begin to choose a second language? Above all, how did the Lord God Our Savior—like the West itself, even the majority of present-day educated humankind on earth—eventually come to speak English?

That biblical story—one of comparative linguistics as much as spiritual revelation—reaches back into the very tatters of history. The earliest extant scrap of any Old Testament dates from the Babylonian captivity in 586 B.C. It is a leather scroll for festive readings at annual Jewish rites, such Mesopotamian times themselves attested to by a cuneiform brick that quotes what King Nebuchadnezzar of Babylon said in praise of his ancient city. Jewish revolts against the Assyrians (168 B.C.) and finally the Romans (135 A.D.) obliterated everything else Hebraic, so that only a stalwart preservation effort by the Masoretes in Tiberius (Galilee) salvaged the recollected Hebrew of the original Old Testament.

But many later Christians wondered whether this so-called Masoretic text was trustworthy. The Masoretes had done their meticulous work from 500 to 1000 A.D., starting five hundred years after the first Christians lived in the catacombs. The oldest known Old Testament manuscript is the *Codex Cairensis* (895 A.D.), and the only complete biblical manuscript is the tenth-century *Aleppo Codex*, so nothing connected the Masoretic text with the lost Talmudic manuscript of half a millennium earlier—until the Dead Sea Scrolls were found in 1947.

St. Jerome, an ascetic monk, devoted his life to the translation of the Latin Vulgate Bible, a text that endured for twelve hundred years in the Catholic Church.

The Dead Sea Scrolls date from the century before Christ's birth to the century after His ministry on earth, more than half a millennium prior to the Masoretes, yet the pots in which they were found amazingly contained every book of the Old Testament but Esther. And they sufficiently reflected the Masoretic text, archeologists have found, to justify the authenticity of the Hebrew Old Testaments on sale today outside the synagogues and churches around the world.

All these early gospel writings were done on papyrus, named for a reed that grows everywhere along the Nile and that provided the first surface (the word *paper* derives from "papyrus") for recording the New Testament. In 112 A.D., Pliny described how the medium was produced by laying out cut strips lengthwise then crosswise, gluing them together with river mud, drying them out, and stone-polishing them to a smooth writing surface. The scribes wrote in many languages—Coptic, Ethiopic, Gothic, Syriac, and Aramaic (supposedly the language Jesus spoke), as well as Latin—but the chief language of the New Testament was initially Greek. The Greek word for "books" is *biblia*—hence, *Bible*—believed to have derived from the city Byblos, which was the commercial center for exporting papyrus around the ancient world. The Greek word for "writing," *scryptos*, becomes the derivative for "scripture" (and the frequent reference in the New Testament to the holy scriptures).

In his effort to get to the original source of the Bible, St. Jerome studied Hebrew from Jewish rabbis.

The great library in Alexandria, Egypt, at the center of the Hellenistic world, had a famous collection of papyrus scrolls before it twice burned. Another library at Pergamum in Asia Minor set out to challenge Egyptian literary dominance; in response, Byblos promptly cut off the Tartars' supply of papyrus. Pergamum craftsmen countered by developing new writing scrolls from treated animal skins; they called the skins *parchment*, again derived from their city's name. Soon enough, parchment from cows and mature sheep remained the most popular medium for medieval scriptures until some enterprising monks introduced a new, more pliable form for the written word: the codex or book.

Scrolls, after all, were written on only one side, with the writing accessible only by rolling the scroll at distant length up or down. But the enterprising monks started cutting the scroll into individual pages and writing on both sides, then binding these pages together sequentially at one edge to form what we now know as a book. To the monks, however, it looked exactly like "a block of wood," for which the Latin word was *quadex*. Hence, the word *codex*. This new format made it so much easier to leaf between the pages, find your place, refer and compare, and even keep your place with a bookmark—or, briefly, your own finger. Try *that* with any scroll!

Actually, try that with a Kindle, which is the latest electronic version of the ancient scroll. It too rolls only up or down, which is why it never offers the reader any page number but instead a percentage of how much of the scroll has been exposed. Referencing and comparing and even making notes is a difficult task, and simply flipping back and forth or sticking a finger between the pages to temporarily hold your place is, of course . . . impossible!

St. Jerome

St. Jerome, an ascetic monk, founded a monastery in the fourth century A.D., lived in a cave, and devoted his life to learning Hebrew and then translating the Latin Vulgate Bible. Courtesy of The Bridgeman Art Library.

"When he chose to leave Rome, or was perhaps forced to leave, he wanted to be in Palestine because this is the land of the birth of Christianity. He wanted to be both in the land as well as exposed to the language of the Bible itself. And therefore he wanted to be as close to the original meaning and sense of revelation that is to be found within the Hebrew Bible."

—David Rosen
Rabbi; Chief Rabbinate of Israel

"Jerome's project is to go back to the Hebrew originals, which is quite a radical idea in his own time. And so he goes to actually learn Hebrew, and of course the only people who can teach him Hebrew are the Jews, and even that idea of Christians learning from the Jews is a bit controversial. But the need for a Latin translation which will be accessible to almost everybody who can read in the West is urgent."

—Alec Ryrie
Professor of the History of Christianity; Durham University, England

"So Jerome makes the journey into Palestine and sets up an ascetic life, almost as a hermit, but with an accompaniment of scholarly women.

"They weren't there just to be secretaries. That I can say for sure. They were there because they wanted to be part of this project of contemplation and study. In the fourth century, in the West, Latin was the spoken language, and the problem was different translations of the Bible, inaccurate in places, collectively known as the Old Latin. Jerome's Vulgate was brought on by the desire to have a standard Latin translation that really was useful, instead of going to one church and hearing the gospel proclaimed one way, then going into another church that used another translation. Latin remained the language of learning. Even as the common spoken languages diverge more, you've got a learned language, and that tradition just keeps going. Learning is conducted in that language, and the heritage of the classics is still available in that language, and we still want to pattern ourselves after them. Vulgate just means 'common.' So, it became the common Bible in Latin. The Vulgate."

—John C. Cavadini
Theologian; University of Notre Dame, Indiana

St. Jerome migrated to Palestine where, with the help of a wealthy Roman heiress and her daughter, Saint Anna and Saint Marcell, he created a monastery where he led an ascetic's life and devoted himself to the creation of an authoritative Latin translation of the Bible.

The freshly thumbing monks felt a deep intellectual attachment to their codices. Eventually they heightened the quality of the page to vellum (made from the more supple skins of fetal lambs and goats) and added artistic decoration with illuminated letters and painted portraits of biblical figures. These were called "miniatures" after the Latin *minium*, the color they used from a red leaf.

As these Bibles grew in size and splendor over the first four centuries of Christendom, so did the babel of languages proliferate in which converts, often the simplest peasantry, professed their belief in Christ as their Savior. A sharp split developed between the educated clergy and the illiterate feudal vassals, who could receive the Word of God only through instruction and readings done from the holy scripture by their priests. Then one dedicated scholar—Eusebius Hieronymus—came forth from the days of Decline and Fall in his native Rome to bring order out of this chaos of variant biblical texts thar were seen to be clouding true belief.

That scholar is known today as St. Jerome, and his statue sits cross-legged before the Italian Embassy along Massachusetts Avenue in the District of Columbia. He is resting a huge Bible on his spread knees, rubbing his bald head with his right hand in grave concentration. He is clad sparingly for his ascetic retreat as an early master of biblical Hebrew and Greek to the Holy Lands, where he spent twenty-two years translating the multilingual writings into a complete version of holy scripture in Latin—his work included all sixty-six books of the Old and New Testaments plus the Apocrypha.

St. Jerome's text became the official Latin Bible of the Roman Catholic Church, known as the Vulgate from *versio vulgata*, "the published version." But it met dissenting judgment early from believers in these so-called Old Latin versions, and St. Jerome was a prickly scholar in controversy. Not until 580 A.D., under Pope Gregory the Great, did the Vulgate emerge as the Latin Bible that spoke for all believers as the "once for all delivered version."

During the ensuing centuries not only did this Latin Bible speak the prevailing Word of God for medieval Christianity, but it also established a rich and magnificent art form. These bound parchment codices became church treasures, with resplendent illuminations and detailed miniatures. The eighth-century Lindisfarne Gospels, now in the British Library, has five so-called "carpet pages" as frontispieces bound by "Billfrith, the anchorite, who forged the ornaments on the outside [binding] and adorned it with gold and with gems and also with gilded—over silver—pure metal."

Such Bibles were so valuable that they were kept chained to the church pulpits to protect against such thieves as Barabas.

In a figurative sense, they were kept chained away from the congregation by their written Latin, a complicated church Latin that was "bureaucratese" designed for ecclesiastical operation of the church's control over sacraments and indulgences. Few enough of the communicants could understand a word of what God was saying to them, except through the interpretation

Venable Bede, a seventh-century monk, translated some of the first Bible verses into the common tongue, known as Old English. Courtesy of The Bridgeman Art Library.

Lindisfarne Gospels

The riches of these Bibles were not only in jewels and precious metals, but in their intellectual property for spiritual guidance. Here, the Gospel of Mark in the Vulgate's Latin is translated, word for word, by the interlinear glosses written in Anglo-Saxon, almost like a tinier hand meticulously following a greater Guide. The vernacular is juxtaposed with the sacred Latin cognates. "The Old English gloss in the Lindisfarne Gospels," David Daniell observes, "is the first extensively written Old English that has survived."

Lindisfarne Gospels folio, courtesy Wikimedia Commons.

in their native language, offered by their clergy. And there existed an often limited view of just how much these serfs really need be told. (See Chaucer's *Pardoner's Tale.*)

What kept the faith alive among the illiterate who were denied any direct knowledge of the Christian Bible in its Latin codex? There still survived the oral tradition—the folk tales of Jesus, Joseph, and Mary, as well as those of Christmas and Easter—that had always spread the Word, though even the parables Jesus preached were largely unknown. There were also plainsong and *Gloria in excelsis deo* or other phrasings from the chants, and always the blessings and *Te Deums* from the high altar. Sporadically there were *Biblia Pauperum* ("The Poor Man's Bible"), done with crude woodblock prints, largely pictorial, with briefer Latin for the priest to interpret or actual worship of the cross in alliterative Old English verse, like *The Dream of the Rood.*

> *Syllic waes se sigebeam   and ic synnum fah*
> ("Beautiful was the victory tree   and I with sins stained")

There were Gothic murmurings *in bookum Psalmo* ("from the psalter") and myths of King Alfred seated enthroned before the encroaching surf to show his foolish counselors that the sea would not obey him as it obeyed God. Alfred also promoted the glossing of the Vulgate, but the entire Anglo-Saxon writings of the *Venable Bede* are sadly lost other than his bleak metaphor of the sparrow flying through the mead hall, in and out—Bede's image of the brevity of mortal life without Christian salvation.

Not until the fourteenth century did a righteous dissenter arise from a small village, Wycliffe-on-Tees in Yorkshire, to expound the words of the

John Wycliffe, 1328–1384, teacher, philosopher, theologian, reformer, translator, and lay preacher. Courtesy of The Bridgeman Art Library.

"Wycliffe was the originator of the Lollard movement. But Wycliffe was rather an academic, a scholar. And it was the next generation, who took his ideas out, his movement of rebellion out into the world."

—Diarmaid MacCulloch
Professor DM, University of Oxford, England

John Wycliffe. Courtesy of The Bridgeman Art Library.

scriptures in English "justified by faith." John Wycliffe attended Oxford, became a doctor of theology around 1373, and was appointed master of Balliol College and warden of Canterbury Hall. His medieval studies were deeply rooted in Latin, but he bravely turned master of the movement by translating the Bible into Chaucerian English. "It seems first that knowledge of God's law should be taught in that tongue that is more known, for this knowledge is God's word."

Churchmen shunned him, but a few loyal scholars took up the task of transcribing his Wycliffe Bible. They were called Lollards, which in German implied "mumblers," presumably of dark intent. But he had some powerful protectors within Parliament, including John of Gaunt, whom Shakespeare had speak the words about "this sceptered isle, this precious stone set in a silver sea," as quoted earlier.

Wycliffe kept arguing that "the New Testament is of full Authority, and open to the understanding of simple men as to the points that have been most needful to salvation." By 1382, the Archbishop of Canterbury had condemned his teachings and declared written translations to be heretical.

In 1374, John Wycliffe taught at Oxford and spoke out against the abuses of the Catholic Church. After his death, his body was disinterred and burned, labeling him forever a heretic.

Wycliffe withdrew from Oxford and died two years later after living in a comfortable parish while his Lollards copied his Wycliffe Bible (of which some 250 manuscripts still exist, six centuries later). The schism brought the Word to the people, but not yet widely enough. Certain priests and those willing to pay were licensed to own an English translation of God's Word, but anybody else found possessing a Wycliffe

The pope returning from Avignon to Rome, carried on a palanquin to a great deal of celebration. Courtesy of the Bridgeman Art Library.

Bible was tried for heresy. The initial question from the inquisitors went something like this: "Do you have a Bible in English, or have you memorized any portion of an English translation?"

At the last, the churchmen wreaked a posthumous vengeance upon Wycliffe in 1428 after the Council of Constance (1414–1416) condemned him along with the Bohemian reformer John Huss. Huss was burned alive at the stake, but Wycliffe had been dead since 1384. So the clerics visited his grave four decades after his death, set fires alongside his makeshift gravestone (inscribed "John de Wyclif"), and exhumed his skeleton. His whited bones were hastily burned and the ashes were scooped up and tossed into the River Swift, a tributary of the Avon. They issued pompous excuses for this desecration—one being to prevent his damned remains from polluting the afterlife—but the better outcome was an anonymous verse that soon sang his praises:

The Avon to the Severn runs,
The Severn to the sea,
And Wycliffe's dust shall spread abroad,
Wide as the waters be.

"The Church had decided there should not be an English Bible. And I think we need to grasp just how odd that was in Europe. In France, in Germany, in Denmark, you could read a Bible in your own language. It wasn't a threat. It was just in this place, this kingdom, where a Bible in the language of the people, in English, simply wasn't available."

—Diarmaid MacCulloch
Professor DM, University of Oxford, England

In truth, the Word was being far more commonly dramatized outside the church—on the play wagons in the medieval town squares, where the so-called Mystery Plays were annually performed in the alternatively religious/raucous Chester and York and Wakefield Cycles. *Mystery* is often a word applied to the inner secrets of medieval guilds, and the term *mystery plays* was appropriately given to these jaunty and elaborately costumed performances done from loose scripture by guild members. They characterized more than a hundred Bible stories in common, often in comic verse, and played them to the hilt in common language for humbling instruction. From Genesis ("Whan Eve span /And Adam delved") to the Crucifixion (Roman soldiers leave Jesus on the cross: "Let him hang there still, /And make faces at the moon"), these dramas gathered the medieval townspeople into a shared passion play, at its best slapstick, most emotional impact.

During the *Second Shepherd's Play* in the Wakefield Cycle, a sheep-thief among the harkening shepherds is discovered, along with his wife, hiding their booty in the cradle. The shepherds toss the culprits in a blanket, which leads seamlessly into the Nativity scene with an angelic choir and pastoral gifts of cherries, a bird, and a ball. Over the off-stage singing of *Gloria in excelsis*, one shepherd recites a lullaby Eucharist to the swaddled Christ child:

> A bird have I brought
> To my bairn
> Hail little tiny mop!
> Of my creed thou are crop [head];
> I would drink in thy cup
> Little day-star.

By papal edict, Wycliffe's ashes were gathered and then poured into the River Swift.

chapter
3

THE BATTLE FOR THE
REFORMATION, 1517–1611

During the fifteenth and sixteenth centuries, knowledge of the holy scriptures erupted from the Dark Ages when the moving Spirit suddenly met moveable type.

Behind the Lollard "mumblings" of Wycliffe already stood a rising tide of belief not just in the true but in the further Word of God. England was slowly stirring, but even more so was Europe—notably the Netherlands, where Rotterdam's Desiderius Eramus had edited the Greek New Testament, translating the scriptures anew into Latin. But nowhere was more turbulence of religious conscience on open display than in the new German university town of Wittenberg, under the elector Frederick the Wise, who kept the young priest Martin Luther under his protection during Luther's intense studies of *sola Christus* ("Christ alone").

Young Martin Luther, born the son of a copper miner, was meant to be a lawyer, but a thunderstorm scared him into becoming a monk. After he'd promised Saint Anne that if she saved him from the lightning, he would take orders, how could he go back on his own word? From such a storm-bent twig, this great oak grew.

Preaching at Wittenberg, Luther argued that Christ's awareness of man's sins caused the Lord

A map of Germany showing Wittenberg, where Luther posted his ninety-five theses. Courtesy of Groberg Films; graphic by Adam Hill.

Johannes Gutenberg, beside a grape press he designed, admiring his print work. Courtesy of The Bridgeman Art Library.

to humble the sinner and thereby seek to save him by God's exercise of His grace. Good works, religious acts—none of these brought or bought a moment's salvation. Only God's grace through His Son's intercession could save sinful humankind. And the corruption deep in the Catholic Church itself—the sale of indulgences, the purchasing of sacred offices and apostolic powers, the amassing of multiple offices by those such as Cardinal Albrecht of nearby Brandenburg—infuriated Luther. He argued that righteousness was a gift that God gave to sinners. A Christian is able to perform good works because faith alone (*sola fide*) has made him righteous. A Christian cannot become righteous simply by doing good works, and surely not by engaging in corrupt practices disguised as good works, which Luther charged the church hierarchy with exploiting.

On October 31, 1517, Luther posted his ninety-five articles against this sale of indulgences and other corrupt practices on the door of the Wittenberg church, which lay outside the boundaries of Cardinal Albrecht's power. But he soon published them in Leipzig, Nuremberg, and Basel, extending his indictment and insisting that the pope could not forgive sins. If he could, why not forgive all sinners without collecting the fees? The signal of alarm regarding the "Reformation" had been sounded, later to turn into the battle cry of the Thirty Years' War across much of Europe.

"And when Martin Luther first appears as a public figure in 1517, when he makes his protests against indulgences, the so-called Ninety-Five Theses, everybody assumes this is part of that same battle over church corruption. What they don't realize is that Luther doesn't have a moral critique of the Church so much as a theological one."

—Alec Ryrie
Professor of the History of Christianity; Durham University, England

Luther was taken by friends into hiding as "Knight George." He paced the floor of his room, ten by fifteen feet, in anxiety and depression, brooding over Satan's corrupting ways. "I know my supporters meant well when they abducted me and brought me here to the Wartburg castle. Now living under a pseudonym, I feel I am a prisoner of my own safety. What will happen to my ministry at the church and the university in Wittenberg while I'm cooped up here? I will not give in to my enemy. I will make it my purpose to fight Satan with 'ink.'"

Over the next ten months, entrapped with Satan gnawing at his troubled soul, Luther took up his pen and translated the New Testament into the common language of his own German people. He used the recently published Greek New Testament by Erasmus, brought out in 1516. Luther translated it into Latin from Erasmus's editing of the variant manuscript of the compiled Septuagint, then the Greek and his Latin were printed in opposing columns, a technique called *Novum Instrumentum*.

As a key to reform, Luther accepted elders for "priests" in his Bible.

But the way, as always, had been prepared. "Those Heretics who pretend that the laity need not know God's law but that the knowledge which priests have imparted to them by word of mouth is sufficient," Wycliffe had pleaded, "do not deserve to be listened to. For Holy Scripture is the Faith of the Church."

Those who believed in the concept of *sola fade* ("sole faith"), which Luther shared with the Lollards, now had the first printing presses available to spread that faith.

Printing in the West had actually begun around 1450 in Germany at Mainz, with experiments in "artificial writing" by a goldsmith named Johannes Gutenberg. He worked in secrecy—and going ever deeper in

Martin Luther remained in a small room for ten months while he translated the Bible from Greek and Hebrew into German in the Wartburg Casltle in Eisenach, Germany.

"Now this led to new interpretations of some crucial passages. A famous one, for instance, is the one about the 'priests' of the church, or are they the elders of the congregation? Erasmus had pointed out that in the old translation of St. Jerome, the passage in the letter of St. James is interpreted in terms of a church hierarchy—God's message is given to the Pope and handed on to bishops and then handed on to priests and then handed on to the ordinary believers. But Erasmus remarked that actually the [Greek] words . . . meant 'elders,' the chosen representatives of the people, not the bishops or priests appointed by the Pope. In other words, by going back to the original sources, Erasmus discovered that the most different way at looking at church hierarchy are the way the faith had to work. It had to work from the bottom upwards, more democratically, you would say today. And that was highly controversial."

—Guido Latre

Professor; University of Louvain and Ghent, Belgium

Desiderius Erasmus. By Hans Holbein the Younger, 1523. Courtesy Wikimedia.

John Wycliffe and other Lollards spreading the word. Courtesy of The Bridgeman Art Library.

A page from a Gutenberg Bible. The master printer wanted a Bible as elaborate as the monks' manuscripts, still much preferred, so he designed moveable type to resemble handwritten letters. Courtesy Wikimedia.

Johannes Gutenberg's invention of the printing press aided the dissemination of tracts and books that further fueled the fires of faith within the common man. They could now read the Bible for themselves.

debt—toward achieving a lasting technological breakthrough. He invented moveable type (without any patent protection) and created the first book printed by a press in the history of the written word. It is also one of the most beautiful pieces of printing art ever produced, and the most valuable printed book in the world. The Gutenberg Bible, printed around 1454–1456, consisted of two hundred copies, twenty of them printed on vellum.

Gutenberg's Bible was printed in Latin using the Vulgate text and was also called the "42-Line Bible" after its folio page size; it was bound in two volumes of 648 and 634 pages, respectively. Today forty-seven existing copies, twelve of them in vellum, tell the sad story of Gutenberg's near triumph and abrupt bankruptcy. He was never an idler or spendthrift, but was only caught up in his trial-and-error "research work" in pursuit of perfection. By 1452, finally ready to print, he borrowed 800 guilders from his associate Johann Fust, then another 800 guilders for what Fust charged in court were "unbridled whims." Now working as Gutenberg's partner, Fust demanded payment—a total of 2,026 guilders—in 1455 when Gutenberg's Bible was partially printed but not yet sold. Fust took over the press, shop, and Bibles and made himself and his family a tidy fortune.

But later scholarship, via X-ray examination of one leaf from the Bible, suggests that Gutenberg was only trying to protect his business secrets. Printings of earlier pages reveal the hand of a craftsman overseeing meticulous practices: the regular recasting of the soft lead type as well as high levels of copper and lead in his ink, applied in small amounts, so that his printed pages have their own chemical "fingerprint."

That chemical fingerprint is missing from the later pages, presumably done under Fust's management. Instead, the later pages are printed in an ordinary carbon-based ink commonly used in the fifteenth-century print shop—another corner cut in final production, since Gutenberg had not passed along his unique ink formula. Gutenberg died penniless in 1468, but Fust and his son-in-law Peter Schoeffer, a disloyal disciple of Gutenberg, prospered within their seized

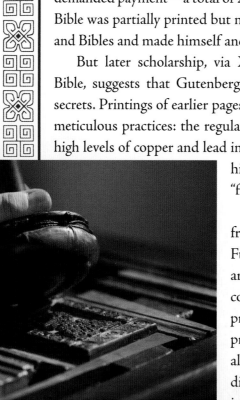

shop as Fust and Schoeffer. One year later, in 1457, they printed their much-lauded Mainz Psalter in three colors on vellum, garnering formidable profits. Gutenberg's name would likely have vanished had not the rector of the University of Paris, Guilluame Fichet, revived his reputation for creating what is most famously known as "The Mazarin Bible." Three years after Johann Gutenberg's obscure death, Fichet recognized him as the inventor of printing.

Luther burns a book titled *Exsurge Domine* in protest of Pope Leo X.

Gutenberg's legacy was already turning Germany into the "cradle of printing" for the *incunabula*, a Latin term for these "infants" among newly printed books. These were the earliest orphaned volumes, sent out into the world before 1500 without even a title page, a listed author, nor hardly any indication of where they might have originated. This was partly deliberate, since so many of these incunabula were Bibles, but were often variant Bibles, vernacular psalters, and translated prayer books. In other words, they were printed in various European languages based on Hebrew and Greek and even Latin texts, but since they were often printed in the vernacular, or native local language, the printer might face a visit from the local police, and, ultimately, the Inquisitors.

Despite such dangers, these incunabula were flooding the market. An international market, profiting on rising sales of Protestant Bibles—and other like-minded publications—printed in seventeen European countries by end of the century. The number of towns with presses grew to 260, with 1,120 printing shops. Forty thousand books in various editions—totaling ten million copies—met with an unforetold explosion in literacy mysteriously at work in a supposedly unlettered world.

Among these abundantly printed books, Luther's German Bible flourished, along with his published sermons and protestant tracts. By 1521, Luther had been brought before church authorities in Augsburg and Leipzig to answer for his failure to acknowledge the authority of the pope. During debate over his offenses at the Diet of Worms, he was required to denounce all of his writings. Luther refused, and his speech of refusal ("I can do no other") was the cry of his heart. "Unless I am convinced by the testimony of the scriptures, or by clear reason (and I do not trust in either the Pope or in councils alone, since it is well known they have often erred and contradicted themselves), I am bound by the scriptures I have quoted and my conscience is captive to the word of God," Luther maintained. "I cannot and will not retract anything, since it is neither safe nor right to go against conscience."

There were other historical influences and occurrences that aided and abetted the Reformation throughout northern Europe during these

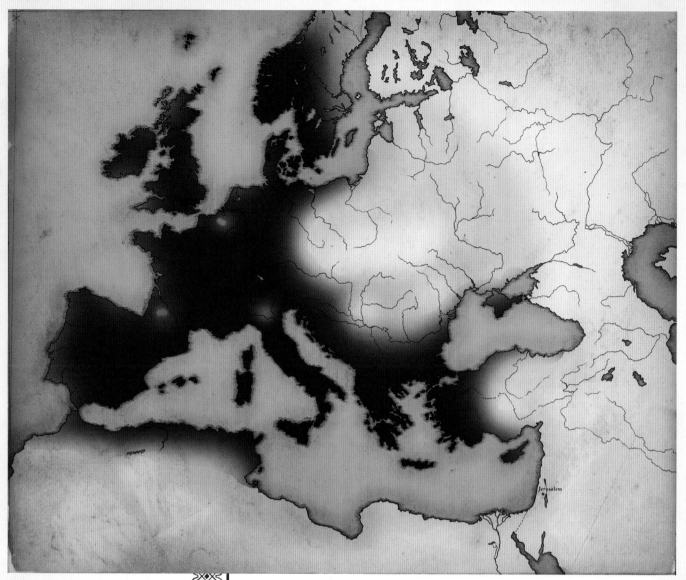

Spread of the Black Death in the fourteenth century. Courtesy of Groberg Films; graphic by Adam Hill.

tumultuous times. The Black Plague periodically devastated the local populations were a death toll of one-third, bringing abrupt changes and differing reaffirmations of religious beliefs outside the clerical hierarchy.

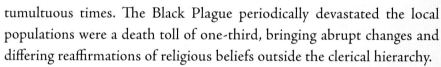

"The Black Death eliminated so many people that it made labor aware of itself as valuable. Their work, all of a sudden, you couldn't just take it for granted. And that creates a kind of social unrest."

—John C. Cavadini
Theologian; University of Notre Dame, Indiana

In 1515 and again a decade later, a Peasants' War arose throughout Germany that supported Martin Luther's reforming practices within the medieval church until the uprising was brutally suppressed.

But somehow this larger unrest did not immediately reach across the English Channel. *The Golden Legend*, the first attempt to print stories from

"The Peasants' War in 1524-25 was a fusion of two things. One is the tradition of rural village-centered revolts in Germany from decades prior—sporadic, some here, some there, none on the scale of what happens in 1524-25. This diffuses with a radicalization, inspired by phrases unleashed in the early German Reformation—phrases like 'freedom of the gospel,' 'the freedom of a Christian,' also direct exposure to scripture itself, and the preaching that is very much part of the same phenomenon. That is what Luther, unintentionally, contributed in the early 1520s."

—Brad Gregory
Professor of Early Modern History; University of Notre Dame, Indiana

the Bible in English, was distributed in 1483, and The Poor Man's Bible (1495) circulated as a pictoral version. But the surprising omission, in light of the early covert distribution of the hand-copied Wycliffe Bible, is that no English Bible was ever printed, either in England itself or abroad, among the prolific, continental incunabula. Instead, the English Bible awaited the arrival of an unheralded literary genius who embarked on an uncommon Puritan act of religious courage.

There were extremely few on the side of those armies—partly comprised of commoners—that were responsible for quelling the revolt.

chapter 4

WILLIAM TYNDALE

Woodblock of William Tyndale. Courtesy of The Bridgeman Art Library.

William Tyndale, likely born in 1494, was a Gloucestershire man, well connected all the way back to the knights and ladies in Richard II's court who served his Bohemian Queen Anne. The Tyndales originated near the River Tyne, which flowed through Northumberland. Like Wycliffe, he attended Oxford—in fact, he attended Magdalen College, where Erasmus had once resided while doing research for his Latin translation of the Greek New Testament, *Novum Intrumentum*. That was likely the newly printed book Tyndale had most recently picked up a year after receiving his master of arts (Oxon) in 1515 to head off for "the other place"—Cambridge, where Erasmus had also later gone to teach as Lady Margaret Professor of Divinity. No record exists of what Tyndale might have learned at Cambridge, but he was at some point ordained a priest, and he eventually proved himself remarkably fluent in eight languages: English, of course, as one of its great writers; both Latin and Greek; later, Hebrew; and French, Italian, Spanish, and German.

But what astounds is how very early on Tyndale chose to put all his learning and intellect into a solitary righteous undertaking at the risk of his own life creating the first English Bible. On one occasion, while serving as tutor to the children of the powerful Lady Anne Poyntz Walsh of Little Sodbury Manor, he was talking with another "learned"

Gloucestershire man—a Catholic priest who cynically unburdened himself "that we're better without God's law," that he much preferred "the pope's law."

At which, reports John Foxe's *Acts and Monuments* of English martyrdom—often called Foxe's *Book of Martyrs*—during the Reformation:

> Maister Tyndall hearing that, answered him, I defy the Pope and all his laws, and said, if God spare my life ere many years, I will cause a boy that driveth the plow, shall know more of the Scripture then thou dost.

He was determined that everybody, down to the plowboy, be allowed to "read" God's Word in his own tongue, the way Tyndale conceived the act of reading itself as inspiring and prophetic. In these early days, "reading" was often considered an act of divination. In his translation of Hebrews 4:12, Tyndale wrote that "the word of God is quick [alive], and mighty in operation, and sharper than a two-edged sword: and entereth through, even unto the dividing asunder of the soul and the spirit, and the joints of the mary [marrow]: and judgeth the thoughts and intents of the heart: neither is there any creature invisible in the sight of it."

Tyndale's first employment after graduation from Oxford was as a personal tutor to the children of the Walsh family.

It was not exactly your average Bible reader. In Tyndale's approach to holy scripture, the Word itself is rendered, in the New Testament phrase, "incarnate" (given a bodily form), but also turned deeply spiritual. Tyndale had an intense awareness of ordinary people's hunger for direct contact with God, which he understood must be couched in real-life, compelling terms, and he had the literary genius to pull it off. That is how he came to write for the first time in plain English: "Give us this day our daily bread."

Tyndale also wrote, for the first time in English, "Blessed are the poor in spirit" (Matt. 5:3), "I am the good shepherd" (John 10:14), "Fight the good fight of faith" (1 Tim. 6:12), and "eat, drink, and be merry" (Luke 12:19), along with many other catch phrases and descriptives that often reach beyond biblical to the proverbial. One example occurs when we talk so knowingly of "the powers that be"—a phrase coined by Tyndale to

"'Let there be light,' 'Eat, drink and be merry,' 'The spirit is willing but the flesh is weak,' all these expressions come from Tyndale and via the King James Bible they have become idioms in the English of today. So you get a vocabulary for your spiritual needs, but you also get a vocabulary for your daily communication. Electric sockets, why do we use the word 'socket' today to describe that electrical appliance? Well, Tyndale had to describe the tabernacle, and he describes it in terms of there shall be bars, boards, pillars and sockets. Now the word 'socket' existed. It was used by carpenters, everywhere in England, but he uses that word because it was accurate and concrete. The sockets for Tyndale were the basis of the pillars and boards of the tents of Israel of the tabernacle around the Arc of the Covenant."

—Guido Latre
Professor; University of Louvain and Ghent, Belgium

describe the Holy Land's Roman occupiers. Such common expressions are recognized widely as we pass through the texts of Tyndale's translations, and many learned them from childhood Bible reading, no matter what profession of faith or religious denomination provided the Bible.

There are three reasons why William Tyndale turned out to be, in a more modern adage, ideal for the job of reforming the faith in the sixteenth century.

First, he took on translating Erasmus's Greek New Testament into an Anglo-Saxon–based English that stood in near tonal contour with the very gist of the Greek itself. Both languages evoked the same visceral responses, whether from the plowboy or the enlightened church dignitary. The Greek was not classical Greek, except in the partial case of St. Luke's Gospel. The Greek was *koiné*—the common, spoken tongue of the Eastern empire that matched the plowboy's succinct, pithy, Anglo-Saxon words. And these words came in short sentences with simple subject-verb-object syntax.

"Tyndale himself says that the Hebrew has this wonderful way of connecting simple sentences with 'and.' And he says English is like that and should do the same. So the Hebrew actually did influence him a lot in making his translation. Moreover, Tyndale remains very close to the original text. He doesn't say, 'God spoke to Elijah,' or 'Elijah listened to God.' You hear in Tyndale's Bible, 'And the word of God came into Elijah.' Now this is a very different concept. Here Elijah receives the Word, is not the active maker or listener. So these constructions come into English and confront scholars and ordinary believers with a different way of thinking."

—Guido Latre
Professor; University of Louvain and Ghent, Belgium

A similar handiness and comparability proved true of his later translations from the Hebrew Old Testament. Hebrew was more complex and poetically stirring, but "the properties of the Hebrew tongue," Tyndale insisted, "agreeth a thousand times more with the English than with the Latin." A wonderful example exists in his famous wording of the twenty-third Psalm: "The Lord is my shepherd; I shall not want. He maketh me to lie down in green pastures" (Ps. 23:1–2).

Second, Tyndale also wrote at the peak of the highest, most lively development of the English language that was newly coming into fruition. His Bible writing was one of the founts of Elizabethan literature. His near contemporary was William Shakespeare, and it is fascinating how sometimes a quotation is still misattributed to the Bard when it really originated with Tyndale. It is clear, particularly from *Hamlet*, that Shakespeare had considerable knowledge of the Geneva Version of the Bible, so dependent on Tyndale's hidden English pen. "Without Tyndale, no Shakespeare," asserts an astute observation that recognizes Tyndale's words find continuous passage into future Bibles, including ultimately the KJV. As in the lament of David (2 Sam. 18:33) for his rebellious son Absalom, as written by Tyndale: "And the king was moved and went up to a chamber over the gate and wept. And as he went thus he said: my son Absalom, my son, my son, my son Absalom, would to God I had died for thee, Absalom, my son, my son."

Another grandly wrought passage occurs in the New Testament—the Christmas story of the shepherds come from their flocks by night to worship the Christ child, told throughout Luke 2. "And they came in haste, and found Mary and Joseph, and the babe laid in the manger." This is vital and clear, but made "memorable," writes David Daniell, an astute scriptural critic, by "placing the 'a' sounds on either side of the central 'Mary': 'and they came with haste' and 'the babe laid in the manger.'" Those are oboe-like triplets of "a" sounds on each side of "Mary," if you count the hidden "a" sound in the word *they*.

A few verses later, Tyndale writes, "And all that heard it, wondered at these things which were told them of the shepherds. But Mary

Tyndale eventually made it to Hamburg, Germany, where he was met by another of his Cambridge associates, Myles Coverdale. They retranslated the lost pages of the Old Testament while staying with a wealthy widow, Margaret Von Emmerson, whose brother was an intimate of Martin Luther.

kept all these things, and pondered them in her heart" (Luke 2:18–19). Again verses are made memorable by the marvelous echoing of *wondered* by *pondered*. At large, folks "wondered" over such things, but Mary inwardly "pondered them." Daniell notes that Tyndale has the Greek dead right—*sunballousa*, which means "thrown together"—but then humanly insists, "Tyndale also knew what it was for a woman to ponder something in her heart."

Third, along with this gift for riveting prose, Tyndale had the complete author's mastery over the rhetoric of his biblical text. He had pledged himself to both clarity and accuracy in his translation, and he managed also to be anglo-inspired in his narrative gift, not abstracted into church Latin. He is also especially careful and effective whenever he quotes Pauline doctrine. He has Paul saying "we have a way in through faith" (Rom. 5:2), where the KJV refers blandly to "access by faith." In Philippians 3:1, he declares "it is a sure thing"—a far cry from the KJV assuring that "it is safe." In Corinthians 2:17, the KJV has Paul calling certain trimmers of God's Word "corrupt," while Tyndale, following the sense of the sailing metaphor in the Greek, condemns those "who chop and change with the word of God." Often his more assertive style sounds surprisingly modern, better than the aloof deportment of the deliberately biblical.

At the close of Matthew 6, the KJV's "Sufficient unto the day is the evil thereof" sounds almost like mistakes were made. Tyndale says it up close and personal: "For the day present hath ever enough of his own trouble." And at any pivotal point, he will not allow a mistaken or misunderstood word to pass his pen. Take Paul's "hymn of love" (see 1 Cor. 13:1): "If I have not love, it profiteth me nothing," translates Tyndale. "So abideth faith, hope, and love: but the greatest of these is love." Enduringly, he correctly interprets the Greek *agape* as "love." The church Latin has *caritas* in these same loci, mildly meaning

Sir Thomas More, 1478–1535, by Hans Holbein. Courtesy of the Bridgeman Art Library.

"charity, caring." Tyndale does not back off from what signifies a bold change in Christian doctrine, even at possible risks of heresy.

And so was Tyndale charged by Sir Thomas More, Lord Chancellor, the most implacable among his enemies in Henry VIII's court.

The bitter dispute between Tyndale and More went on for several years in correspondence of many volumes, largely scriven by More. In 1528, More applied to Cuthbert Tunstall, bishop of London, for permission to read heretical books so that he might vilify Tyndale as worse than Luther. The next year, More published his *Dialogue Concerning Heresies*, in which he attacked what he considered the most essential of Tyndale's doctrinal interpretations, such as his substitution of the sensual *love* for the chaste *charity*. Other targets were Tyndale's belief in religious rule residing in the "congregation" as opposed to More's one true "church." Tyndale's governance, following Erasmus, was by "senior" congregants, those "elders" who should replace More's rule by the "priest," and above all, Tyndale wrote that Christians must themselves "repent" of their sins, not simply "do penance." That way lay the sale of indulgences and other corrupt ecclesiastical practices, Tyndale fervently argued.

Tyndale's *An Answer unto Sir Thomas More's Dialogue* criticized perversion of the scriptures by More and noted his total silence on the many corruptions of the church. This brought More back with *Confutation of Tyndale's Answer* that went on for six volumes and half a million words, yet was never really finished. Almost every page scorns Tyndale for such foul acts as "discharging a filthy foam of blasphemies out of his brutish beastly mouth."

For his own safety, Tyndale went abroad after 1523, once Cuthbert Tunstall refused his request to render the New Testament in the plowboy's English. Secretly, he was already far along toward that goal, but he knew he had to cross the English Channel to find a reliable printer. There were rumors of possible visits to nearby Wittenberg for sessions with Luther, but his first recorded business was in Cologne with Peter Quentell to print sheets of his New Testament up through Matthew 22. A slim volume was printed in quarto size, but Quentell's shop was promptly raided by the city police of the Inquisition. Tyndale subsequently moved up the Rhine to the safe Lutheran city of Worms with what remaining pages of Matthew he had rescued. "Ask, and it shall be given you; seek, and ye shall find; knock, and it shall be opened unto you" (Matt. 7:7) Those clarion calls still move the English-speaking believer today, though he is forewarned:

The printing of the Tyndale Bible and other tracts took place in Belgium and Germany. The Plantin-Moretus museum and print shop in Antwerp was likely an actual printing location for Tyndale's works. William Tyndale personally supervised the printing of his works.

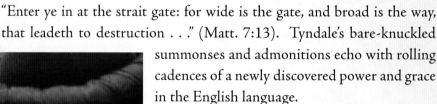

Original page of Tyndale Bible (Boyd K. Packer, owner). Courtesy, The Church of Jesus Christ of Latter-day Saints. Kimball Ungerman, photographer.

Tyndale Bibles were smuggled into England from Belgian and German printshops.

"Enter ye in at the strait gate: for wide is the gate, and broad is the way, that leadeth to destruction . . ." (Matt. 7:13). Tyndale's bare-knuckled summonses and admonitions echo with rolling cadences of a newly discovered power and grace in the English language.

By 1526, a small printer in Worms—son of the "Gutenberg" Peter Schoeffer—had printed Tyndale's New Testament in the smaller octavo size, unembellished, the same pocket size (readily hidden) that Tyndale used for all his future books. Merchants used bales of cotton and seed to smuggle the copies down the Rhine into English and Scottish ports, and Antwerp's "pirate" printers added their cheapened share.

Back in England, Cuthbert Tunstall went ballistic—"in the english tongue that pestiferous and moste pernicious poison dispersed throughout all our dioces of London in great number." He stacked copies of Tyndale's New Testament in front of St. Paul's, preached against them on October 27, 1526, and burned the lot. But the octavo-size New Testament was already out, everywhere. Tunstall's chaplain assured him they'd burned "many hundreth, both heir and beyond the see." Agents bought up rogue printings abroad, but that only meant more quick cash for Antwerp

merchants without having to risk shipping costs. Today, we have only one remaining complete copy of Tyndale's 1526 New Testament, discovered at the Stuttgart Lanesbibliothek in 1999. But the printed Word, born of that moveable type that created hidden hordes of enough stitched scripture to put pages into the plowboy's hands, has never stopped spreading.

The spread of the Bible is equally due to the miraculous triumph of language that Tyndale achieved in secret, creating the major content of far-future English Bibles. He kept revising his New Testament while continuing his translation work on the Old Testament for a year in Hamburg, where he was rumored to have arrived by shipwreck and to have lost all of his papers and books. But it is difficult to put much credence in the stories of this reputed seaside calamity, because Tyndale continued to labor at publishing sharp defenses of his beliefs in *The Parable of the Wicked Mammon* and *The Obedience of a Christian Man*. His tracts were as widely read as they were officially condemned, deemed treasonous as well as heretical. "Let it not make thee despair neither yet discourage thee O reader," *Obedience* opens its plea, "that it is forbidden thee in pain of life and goods or that it is made breaking of the King's peace or treason unto His Highness to read the word of thy soul's health." Henry VIII was very much on Tyndale's mind, and from this time forward, Tyndale was very much on the King's mind as well.

Tyndale finally moved to Antwerp, where all his books after 1528 were published by solid, reputable printers, even if they never mentioned their author's name and used pseudonyms themselves. "Hans Luft of Marlborow" brought out both *Mammon* and *Obediance*. It was actually a large house run by Martin de Keyser, also known as Martin

It is rumored that while traveling from Belgium to Germany, Tyndale was shipwrecked off the coast of Holland. Conjecture is that his entire translation of the first five books of the Old Testament was lost at sea.

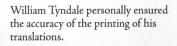

William Tyndale personally ensured the accuracy of the printing of his translations.

l'Empereur. The real Hans Luft was Martin Luther's printer in Wittenberg, so the whole setup has all the trappings of a printer's inside joke.

Tyndale was living under the protection of Thomas Poyntz at the English House in Antwerp, where a dissenting minister named John Rogers arrived to serve as chaplain to resident English merchants in 1534. Tyndale could work there to complete his Bible in relative safety from harassment, since Poyntz was related to the powerful Lady Anne Poyntz Walsh of Little Sodbury Manor, for whose family Tyndale had once been a tutor. By 1530, Tyndale had finished his translation of the Pentateuch, printed again by "Hans Luft of Marlborow" and on sale as a single volume or as five separate books, each with prologues by "W. T." Introducing Genesis, Tyndale explained how "we may apply the medicine of the scripture, every man to his own sores, unless we intend to be idle disputers, and brawlers about vain words, ever gnawing at the bitter bark without and never attaining to the sweet pith within, and persecuting one another for defending of lewd imaginations and fantasies of our own invention." He had an unwinking eye for the destructive controversy that More had unleashed against his own veritable mission in life.

Four years later, he had ready a host of revisions for his New Testament. But his 1526 Worms edition was still selling well in Great

The Book of Common Prayer. Courtesy of Joe and Jeanne Groberg Collection, on loan to Special Collections, Brigham Young University–Idaho Library. Kimball Ungerman, photographer.

Britain, even the small-sized, pirated excerpt of his Cologne Matthew. The widow of the pirating Antwerp printer hired a truant English editor named George Joye to help her put out yet another rogue printing of his Cologne Matthew. Joye not only cooperated, but took it upon himself to alter Tyndale's use of the word *resurrection* to "the life after this life." Besides being a gross violation of Tyndale's text, Joye's anonymous change raised the whole theological debate over the Resurrection, then much disputed among the Reformers. Tyndale now had to save his own writings from distortion by false witness on the part of an editor serving a piratical printer.

Tyndale did so in his prologue to his 1534 New Testament. He castigated Joye for his meddling and told him he was free to foist off his erroneous ideas under his own name, but not Tyndale's (though Tyndale was still not admitting to public use of his own real name, only his initials!). "W. T." further elaborated on how his Hebraic reading in the Old Testament had deepened and enriched his understanding of the New Testament.

Anne Boleyn reading the Bible. Courtesy of The Bridgeman Art Library.

Altogether a much-corrected and welcome improvement over his earlier edition, the 1534 edition well printed as a handsome, small volume by Martin de Keyser with notable additions to the understanding of New Testament life. *Revelations* is illustrated with twenty-two woodcuts depicting the chaos and havoc of those distressing events described therein. Fifteen later pages provide forty Old Testament readings in English, keyed to the daily calendar of services at Salisbury Cathedral. Here lie the roots of the Book of Common Prayer, which would be the great liturgical contribution of Archbishop Thomas Cranmer to worship in the Church of England. Cranmer later lost his head during the reign of Bloody Mary, ever himself a stalwart support within the royal court for the Reformers.

More copies of this New Testament survive than those of Tyndale's 1526 edition. It may have enjoyed greater unofficial tolerance, as its unstoppable distribution proved its increasing popularity. It is rumored within the court

"King Henry certainly was influenced by this little book, *The Obedience of a Christian Man.* One of the Ladies-in-Waiting to Anne Boleyn was caught reading this book, so Anne had to protect her, and of course got the help of Henry to protect this poor woman. This is the moment when Henry reads the tract himself and concludes, 'This is a book that all the princes in Europe should read.'

"It is a very reassuring book for him because princes can continue to rule by divine right, even Tyndale didn't deny that, but they would also rule by the consent of the population. It stated that ordinary readers of the Bible, who would form their own opinion, were of no danger to the unity of the state because they would still live in a hierarchic orderly society.

"And this actually became the great secret of the reign of Henry's daughter, Queen Elizabeth I. She ruled by divine right, and she was proud of this, but also with popular consent."

—Guido Latre
Professor; University of Louvain and Ghent, Belgium

To mitigate an otherwise painful death, Tyndale was strangled before being burned.

that Henry VIII was inclined toward greater interest in the sole scripture that had sent so many Protestants retreating into exile abroad. One copy of this New Testament belonged to Queen Anne Boleyn herself. The Queen's name is not secretly written somewhere inside this prohibited book, but outside on the edges of the pages, "BOLEYN," where it can readily be seen. Her New Testament resides today on display at the British Museum.

Queen Anne's protestant influence on the king was made vividly clear when one of her retinue was found reading a Tyndale pamphlet.

Actually, the greatest survival of Tyndale's biblical writings lies further on, in its continuance over the next five centuries, even until today. The agreed estimate of the debt in words owed William Tyndale by those who "translated" the New Testament for the King James Version is 83 percent.

chapter
5

TYNDALE'S FATE

"Lord, open the king of england's eyes!"

F or all the courage he mustered in Antwerp as a religious self-exile, Tyndale felt sorely, often mortally tried. He was unhappy in his poverty and suffered from hunger, cold, thirst, the absence of friends, and "the great danger wherewith I am everywhere encompassed." He endured because he yet "hoped with my labors to do honour to God."

Tyndale had already seen his closest friends back in England suffer for having been among the first readers of his 1526 English New Testament. In 1528, Cambridge scholar Thomas Bilney had been arrested for heresy and promptly recanted. But despite his gentleness of spirit, Bilney could not abide his own apostasy. He handed out Tyndale Bibles and, two years later, was burned at the stake.

Tyndale was also writing to his earlier associate in the Lowlands, John Frith, who had been sent to Newgate Prison in 1531. Tyndale, writing to him as "Jacob," exhorts

Thomas Bilney, "Little Bilney," preached from the English Bible in defiance of the Catholic Church.

"One of the first martyrs of the English Reformation, [Thomas] Bilney had exactly the problem of having gone back on his Evangelical faith. He gave way. And what did he do then, in his agony? He went back to the place where he had originally preached his Evangelical doctrine, despite the fact he had recanted."

—Diarmaid MacCulloch
Professor DM, University of Oxford, England

Sir Thomas Cromwell, 1385–1540. Chief Minister to King Henry VIII, 1532–1540. Portrait by Hans Holbein the Younger. Courtesy Wikimedia.

Frith scripturally to take courage in the face of his coming martyrdom, assuring him of his wife's and family's support from exile. Frith writes Tyndale that "for his learning and judgment in scripture, he is more worthy to be promoted than all the bishops in England." But Frith too was soon executed in 1533.

An uncertain Tyndale was willing to speak of his misery as early as 1531 to Stephen Vaughan, who was Henry VIII's factor in the Netherlands. Vaughn had been commissioned by Thomas Cromwell, Archbishop of Canterbury, to contact Tyndale. It would appear that Henry VIII now felt his peace might be safer with Tyndale returned to England. In January, Vaughn got a letter through to Tyndale, offering safety if Tyndale would agree to meet with him.

Tyndale initially refused, suspicious of entrapment. But by April, he was willing to meet with Vaughn in a field outside Antwerp. Tyndale declared his strong loyalty to the king. Vaughn reported back to Cromwell and argued that he wrote to bring the gift of Christ's living words to his king's subjects. Did his king fear them more than the difficult clergy, against whom Tyndale professed he wrote to protect his king? Meeting secretly with Vaughn again in May, Tyndale made a grand promise to him. "I assure you, if it would stand with the king's most gracious pleasure to grant only a bare text of the scripture to be put forth among the people . . . be it of the translation of what person soever shall please his majesty, I shall immediately make faithful never to write more . . . but immediately to repair unto his realm, and there most humbly submit myself at the feet of his royal majesty, offering my body to suffer whatever pain or torture, yea, what death his grace will." It was only what the Holy Roman Emperor Charles V of Spain and other Christian princes had already done for their own people.

After a third meeting where similar promises were exchanged, Vaughn wrote Cromwell twice on Tyndale's behalf, but to no avail. Tyndale's dark suspicions were correct. "The powers that be" were again shifting their grounds to match rising, turbulent religious convictions within Henry's court. Henry VIII might have been brought to approve an English Bible, but he could not stomach a Puritan like Tyndale himself. The next emissary would come from Sir Thomas More—Sir Thomas Elyot, sent to arrest Tyndale.

But Tyndale's entrapment still required a Judas. One such stopped inside the English House during the spring of 1535—Henry Phillips, a transient, debauched young Englishman who insinuated himself into Tyndale's trusting company. A sinner claiming an interest in this new English Bible, he was also in want of a quick loan. Phillips had gambled away funds entrusted to him by his father to be paid in London and then had fled, full of scheming self-pity, to the Lowlands. Tyndale loaned him a pittance, but Phillips had arranged with church authorities to deliver up Tyndale for real blood money. Those arrangements had most likely been made through the new bishop of London, John Stokesley, who had revived the practice of burning heretics, along with their books.

On May 21, Phillips duped Tyndale into leaving the English House, and the poor man was arrested in the alley so easily "that they pitied to see his simplicity when they took him." He was imprisoned in the castle of Vilvorde, outside Brussels, for the next sixteen months under the prosecutorial eye of the procurer-general, Pierre Dufief, a cruel and avaricious zealot. Dufief shared any convicted heretic's confiscated property, and he started compiling evidence against Tyndale by having Phillips, always at hand, produce summaries of his heretical English works in church Latin.

The English merchants in Antwerp, led by Thomas Poyntz, fought hard for Tyndale's release, sending appeals to Henry VIII's court. This panicked Phillips, who not only saw his pay-off vanishing but feared certain remarks he'd made in his own letters to England would be seen as insults to the king. If Cromwell ever saw them, Phillips would likely be sent to the Tower of London for execution. "The king's grace," Poyntz pressed forward, "should have of him [Tyndale] at this day as high a treasure as any man living . . . there be not many perfecter men this day living, as knows God." Cromwell, back in the struggle for Tyndale's return, had written two privy councilors in Brabant. These letters, used by

William Tyndale stayed in hiding in Antwerp, Belgium, to avoid spies and bounty hunters. Ultimately betrayed by a "friend," he was arrested by Belgian authorities and kept in Vilvorde Prison for sixteen months prior to his execution by strangling and immolation.

Chief Inquisitor Jacobus Latomus, 1475–1544. Courtesy Wikimedia.

Poyntz to lobby his tangled contacts within Brussels, were succeeding. He was told Tyndale would be released into his custody.

So Phillips promptly denounced Poyntz as Tyndale's companion in heresy. Poyntz was placed under house arrest, with Phillips always at the door whenever the Inquisitors arrived. Alerted to the danger he was in, Poyntz fled to England. That ended any hope for Tyndale's freedom, and Phillips ran away across Europe to meet his impoverished death in 1542, everywhere denounced as a thief and false informer.

The flight of Phillips did not stop Tyndale's trial from inexorably proceeding before seventeen commissioners, led by three chief accusers, under the greatest grand inquisitor in Europe, Jacobus Latomus. Tyndale conducted his own defense, though his fate was already sealed. Latomus was interested only in attempting to return Tyndale to Christian orthodoxy in order to save his soul before burning his body. He pressed an immense interrogatory upon Tyndale, producing six books of detailed answers from the accused, who maintained, *"Sola fides justificat apud Deum"* ("faith alone justifies before God") and referred oft to *"Clavis intelligentiae salutaris sacrae scriptuae"* ("the key to the understanding of scripture as salvation"). In the process, Latomus could not avoid reproducing much of what Tyndale had previously written over his lifetime. Latomus respected his condemned prisoner as a great scholar and brought forth his "last, lost" book in detail, as David Daniell notes. We have access to that book in the Latin of the Inquistion, writes Daniell, "all of a piece with everything else he published, in its logical development, clarity, and, above all, absolute dependence on, and great knowledge of, Scripture, especially Paul."

The tragedy is that this "last, lost" book—couched in the Latin testimony from Tyndale's own heresy trial—was the only certainty Tyndale

Tyndale's Letter from Vilvorde

"I beg your Lordship, and that by the Lord Jesus, that if I am to remain here through the winter, you will request the Commissary to have the kindness to send me from the goods of mine which he has, a warmer cap, for I suffer greatly from a cold in the head, and am afflicted with a perpetual cough, which is much increased in this cell. A warmer coat also, for this which I have is very thin: a piece of cloth too to patch my leggings: and I ask to be allowed to have a lamp in the evening, it is indeed wearisome sitting alone in the dark. But most of all, I beg and beseech your clemency to kindly permit me to have the Hebrew Bible, the Hebrew Grammar, and Hebrew Dictionary, that I may pass the time in that study. But if any decision has been taken concerning me to be carried out before winter I will be patient, abiding the will of God to the glory and grace of my Lord Jesus Christ, whose Spirit I pray, may ever direct your heart. Amen. William Tyndale."

William Tyndale. Courtesy Wikimedia.

had that his words might somehow survive. He had been kept in the dark, incommunicado, during his imprisonment at Vilvorde, even as he begged for "a lamp in the evening; it is indeed worrisome sitting alone in the dark."

Tyndale heard not one word of English during his entire incarceration among the Flemish nor at his trial, which was conducted in Church Latin. During the preceding seven years, he had published two editions of his New Testament along with his Pentateuch in pocket-sized English books that crossed the Channel as hidden contraband in smugglers' ships. But from 1526, when his first English scriptures were condemned as heretical, he knew his books were destined for the Church's roaring burn pile.

He had left behind at the English House a manuscript of fourteen historical chapters of the Old Testament, translated into English, but these must surely have been seized. Tyndale went to his martyrdom in ignorance about whether his fundamental achievement at Worms and Antwerp would burgeon through furtive reading down in the country dells and within the city mews, long enough for his fragmented English Bible to gain its own lasting shelf life. He never knew if they would all join him in feeding the constant flames.

Death of William Tyndale, portrayed in woodblock. Courtesy of *Foxe's Book of Martyrs.*

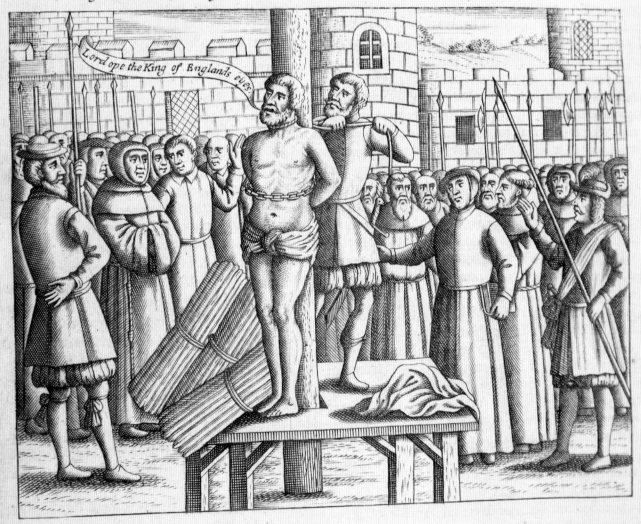

The Martyrdome of Master William Tindall in Flanders, by Vilvord Castle.

Lord ope the King of Englands eyes

October 6, 1536, William Tyndale's life was ended by strangulation and his body was burned.

In August 1536, William Tyndale was condemned as a heretic and publicly degraded from his priesthood the same day in a grim ceremony for which Dufief was paid the costs of arranging the elaborate ritual. A far larger assembly was gathered on an early October morning, customarily believed to be October 6, before a stake, brushwood, and logs that were arranged as a pyre in an open town space. Tyndale was brought out, full of fair greetings to those in attendance. Then a chain was wrapped around his neck with its trailing links wrenched over the top of the stake. He gave the cry that John Foxe reports: "Lord, open the King of England's eyes!" He was not burned alive. As a mark of respect for his distinction as a scholar, Tyndale was garroted with the chain pulled link-tight across his throat, strangled to death before the logs were set aflame.

Cromwell's agent John Hutton, acting on the Archbishop's sympathies, wrote from Brabant that December, "They speak much of the patient sufferance of Master Tyndale at the time of his execution." In 1550, Roger Ascham, tutor to Princess Elizabeth, rode through Vilvorde and noted: "At the town's end is a notable solemn place of execution, where worthy William Tyndale was unworthily put to death."

chapter 6

COVERDALE'S BIBLE AND MATTHEW'S BIBLE

Tyndale's agonizing work of ages had not gone missing. The very year of Tyndale's arrest, Miles Coverdale—a milder English colleague in Antwerp—brought out the first complete English Bible. Coverdale's Bible was imported and legally sold in England, then reprinted by a London publisher, James Nicholson of Southwark, and dedicated to King Henry VIII. This was made possible in large part by a secret rescue of Tyndale's manuscripts from his quarters at English House, despite Pierre Dufief's illegal raid on Tyndale's premises before his protracted trial for heresy.

From Belgium and German print shops, Bible manuscript pages were concealed and then smuggled to the docks of England, then on to print binderies. The bound Bibles were then sold on the black market.

"Sure I am," Coverdale professes, "that there cometh more knowledge and understanding of the Scriptures by their sundry translations than by all the glosses of our sophistical doctors."

Miles Coverdale, though a whole-hearted reformer willing to face exile for his beliefs, was far less confrontational than Tyndale. Born in York, he became an Augustinian friar before moving to the house of his order in Cambridge, where he began, as he wrote early to Thomas Cromwell, "to taste of holy scripture." This again points to how rarely even religious

Myles Coverdale

John Hooker of Exeter, a servant of Miles Coverdale, wrote of him: "He did most worthily perform the office committed to him: he preached continually upon every holy day, and did read most commonly twice in the week in some one church or other within this city. He was, after the rate of his livings, a great keeper of hospitality, very sober in diet, godly in life, liberal to the poor, and courteous to all men, full of humility, abhorring covetousness, and an enemy of all wickedness and wicked men, whom he shunned, and whom he would in no wise shroud or have in his house or company."

Eighteenth-century engraving from a 1533 portrait of Coverdale from the 1837 edition of Coverdale's *Letters of the Martyrs*. Courtesy Wikimedia.

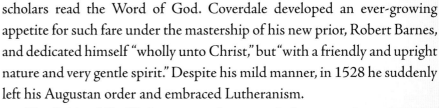

scholars read the Word of God. Coverdale developed an ever-growing appetite for such fare under the mastership of his new prior, Robert Barnes, and dedicated himself "wholly unto Christ," but "with a friendly and upright nature and very gentle spirit." Despite his mild manner, in 1528 he suddenly left his Augustan order and embraced Lutheranism.

The Spirit of God "is in some a vehement wind, overturning mountains and rocks," wrote Coverdale's tutor, John Bale, "but in [Coverdale] it is a still small voice comforting wavering hearts. His style is charming and gentle, flowing limpidly along: it moves and instructs and delights."

Coverdale approached his own English translation of the Bible in exactly this accommodating fashion. Depending on "five sundry interpreters" to help him, he wrote *Unto the Christian Reader* in 1535—"not only in Latin, but also the Douche [German] interpreters: whom (because of their singular gifts and their special diligence in the Bible) I have been the more glad to follow in the most part." Among other aides to translation (several of whom specialized in Swiss-German and Latin), he included Martin Luther, whose German Bible was out by 1532; the Latin Vulgate; Tyndale's English New Testament; and the first fourteen books Tyndale had completed in translating the Hebrew Old Testament. These fourteen books had been mysteriously recovered, despite Dufief's arrest and imprisonment of Tyndale.

So Coverdale's Bible was basically his adaptation of previous translations, supplemented by necessary contributions of his own, which has led some critics to see him as hardly an originalist and variously "quaint." C. S. Lewis called him "a rowing-boat among battleships," but allowed that such status gave him the freedom "to select and

"Myles Coverdale took Tyndale's New Testament, joined it to the books of the Old Testament they had translated together, and published the first ever English Bible with the Old and New Testaments under one cover."

combine by taste." "Fortunately," concludes Lewis, "his taste was admirable." Out of his admiration for the German multiple-compounding interpreters, Coverdale also liked to coin and straddle compound neologisms in English. Some of his contributions were inspired, including "winebibber," "loving kindness," "saving health," and even "tender mercies"—but what is to be made of a vocal contortion like "unoutspeakable" in Romans 8:26?

In adopting Tyndale's New Testament, Coverdale honored Tyndale's crucial choices of Christ's Word in support of Pauline doctrine, such as *congregation, elder,* and, above all, *love* as the greatest of these after faith and hope. But he does sometimes use *penance* for *repentance,* in his own belief that doing penance must encompass direct contact of one's whole being with God. This seems to be sufficiently compatible reasoning between Tyndale and Coverdale, since the two men appear to have become close after Coverdale too had exiled himself to Antwerp. Coverdale often checked English proof for Martin de Keyser ("Hans Luft of Marlborow," Tyndale's foremost printer in Antwerp).

Coverdale adopted Tyndale's English Old Testament through 2 Chronicles, though he did mildly alter the seventh commandment to read, "Thou shalt not break wedlock." After that, Coverdale did his translating from the Latin of the Vulgate. He sometimes did well with translating the prophets. "Seek the Lord while he may be found, call upon him while he is nigh" is his in Isaiah 55:6, almost as it survives in KJV, which only added "ye." But his genuine triumph came in his sweetly and smoothly flowing translations of the Latin Psalms that carried forward to the Great Bible, which he also edited, and eventually to the KJV.

Title page of the Coverdale Bible. Woodcut, 24 × 16.7 cm, British Library, London. Courtesy Wikimedia Commons.

David Daniell makes an historical point: "The Church of England at worship sang or said Coverdale every day for over four hundred years," since one of his psalms had always been part of the liturgy in the Book of Common Prayer until the very day the Revised Standard Version (RSV) arrived in the racks of the church pews, with its acrid modernization of the Psalms. Daniell argues that this change brought about more than an historical linguistic stop, since Coverdale's words were compositionally more musical and always "singable."

Psalm, of course, is the Greek word for the lyrics that accompany the melody brought forth by a group of musical instruments. They are the words to the holy music, the text that is to be sung during services. Fortunately, writes Daniell, echoing Lewis, "Coverdale's Psalms are naturally musical."

Coverdale's psalms were crafted to suit the vocal outpouring of the choir and the chorusing reply of the congregation. Daniell cites Coverdale's Second Psalm— "Why do the heathen furiously rage together: and why

do the people imagine a vain thing?" In contrast, the more modern RSV rendition features an awkward plural: "Why are the nations in turmoil? Why do the people hatch their futile plots?"

Many people cannot read Coverdale's words without "hearing in their heads Handel's bass aria from the *Messiah*," but who could sing, asks Daniell, all those "spitting 't' sounds of 'hatch' . . . 'futile' . . . 'plot'"? The words may make more modern and accurate sense, but they don't thrum smoothly as the *n*s do through "imagine a vain thing." Musicality can bring the least phrase alive in an oratorio. In Psalm 115, Coverdale's "Not unto us, O Lord, not unto us" trills enlightened refusal, compared to its clunky rewrite in the RSV: "Not to us, O Lord, not to us. . . ." Coverdale understood the flow that alternates strong and soft stresses so that the congregation can join together in shared song. It is far easier to sing "the firm! -a -ment show! -eth his hand! - i - work" from Coverdale than mouth four strong modern stresses producing a cacophonic "heav! - en's vault! makes! known!" Often the grace truly lies in the grace notes.

Finally, Coverdale's Bible was the first to separate out the fourteen (or fifteen) "hidden" books between the Old and New Testaments. Typically, he did this with great care: "These books (good reader) which are called Apocrypha, are not judged among the doctors to be of like reputation with the other scripture, as you may perceive by St. Jerome in '*Epistola ad Paulinium.*' And the chief cause thereof is this: there be many places in them, that seem to be repugnant unto the open and manifest truth in other books of the Bible. Nevertheless, I have not gathered them together to the intent that I would have them despised, or little set by, or that I should think them false. For I am not able to prove it: Yea, I doubt not verily, if they were equally conferred with the other scripture (time, place and circumstances in all things considered) they should neither seem contrary, not be untruly and perversely alleged." He goes on, with another equal hundredweight of tact, to suggest, "let the plain text be thy guide, and the spirit of God (which is the author thereof) shall lead thee in all truth."

Coverdale's Bible is a handsome book, in both folio and quarto, with 158 pictures, highly decorative illuminations, and serial illustrations. Its title page also marks the first appearance of Henry VIII amidst the hierarchy of the church. God is named by His glowing initials of the *Tetragrammaton* (Hebrew for God) at the very top, and New and Old Testament figures follow in biblical vignettes. But royally

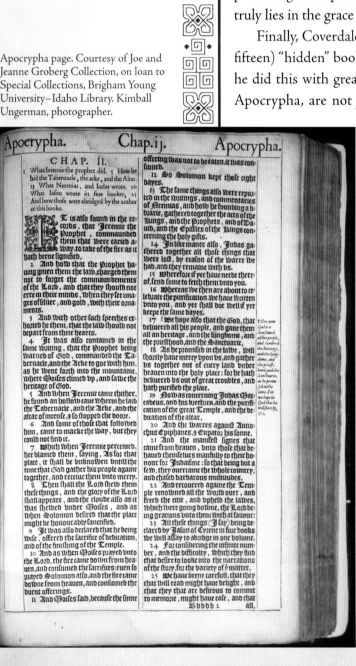

Apocrypha page. Courtesy of Joe and Jeanne Groberg Collection, on loan to Special Collections, Brigham Young University–Idaho Library. Kimball Ungerman, photographer.

seated at the bottom of the page is King Henry VIII himself—from a handsome portrait by Hans Holbein the Younger—as a somewhat modest monarch, distributing "thy words" and "the gospel" to the clergy and nobles. This English translation was thus licensed by the king and clearly belonged respectably on top of any important Tudor desk. Indeed, there has been considerable speculation under whose auspices Coverdale chose to put this volume together. Archbishop Thomas Cromwell, newly appointed Vice Regent, surely sponsored the Holbein image "as a public means of validating Henry's claim to govern without clerical intercession as the sole intermediary between temporal society and the divine order." But the new Archbishop of Canterbury, Thomas Cranmer, might also well have been involved, since Cranmer had tried to launch a Bishops' Bible as far back as 1533, though the recalcitrant bishops claimed "as yet they had no leisure."

Thomas Cranmer, 1489–1556. Adviser to King Henry VIII, Archbishop of Canterbury and Protestant martyr under Queen Mary. Courtesy of The Bridgeman Art Library.

But the greatest mystery remains: Who saved that cache of Tyndale manuscripts, especially his Old Testament translations, from Dufief's intrusive searches and their surefire burning by the Inquisition? The most likely soul to have removed these papers from English House was its chaplain, John Rogers. He would then not only be able to provide them to Miles Coverdale, but also to use them himself in his own publication of another "Tyndale Bible" that he created with the Antwerp printer Matthew Crom in 1537. Rogers's "Tyndale Bible" is likewise a handsome folio, printed in black letter in double columns, with its own hidden secrets. A printing of fifteen hundred copies was distributed across the Channel, underwritten by two reforming merchants in London, Richard Grafton and Edward Whitchurch. All Tyndale's biblical writings finally lay bound, untampered with by gentler hands like those of Coverdale, between two covers.

Lord receive my spirit

Burning death of John Rogers.
Courtesy of Foxe's *Book of Martyrs*.

John Rogers emerges from this venture as another of those reforming church dignitaries who valiantly risked exile abroad.

He too had gone to Cambridge, earning his bachelor of arts degree at Pembroke Hall in 1526. Rogers led a London parish before he slipped overseas to become chaplain of English House and there married a Flemish kinswoman of Jacob van Meteren, who had sponsored Coverdale's English Bible. So Rogers was deeply enmeshed in the reform movement during the six years he spent in Antwerp.

But in 1540, Rogers moved with his family to Wittenberg, where he matriculated and studied under the famous Lutheran scholar Philip Melanchthon. Rogers became a German cleric, far up in the Ditmarsch region, where he had some difficulty communicating with his rural congregation, though Melanchthon backed him to the hilt: "a learned man . . . with a noble character . . . he will be careful to live in concord with his colleagues . . . his integrity, trustworthiness and constancy in every duty make him worthy of the love and support of all good men."

Before such wanderings Ditmarsch, however, Rogers bravely guided "Matthew's Bible"—as the book became surreptitiously known—through the printing press to its immediate success once shipped ashore in England. His noteworthy achievement was to bring out this biblical volume less than twelve months after Tyndale had been martyred with the wish, "Lord, open the king of England's eyes!" on his dying lips. Cromwell, who had lately become Henry VIII's powerful vice-regent for ecclesiastical affairs, actively encouraged bishops to order copies for their churches. He had also been able to facilitate its dedication to the king—"To the most noble and gracious Prince King Henry the eight"—as well as to obtain a royal license for this English version of the Bible. Right on the title page, it said, "Set forth with the King's most gracious license."

Matthew's Bible was promptly popular. On August 4, 1537, Thomas Cranmer—now archbishop himself—wrote Cromwell, "So far as I have read thereof I like it better than any other translation heretofore made." He warned there would be "some snubs, many slanders, lies and reproaches," but said these masked the hidden objection that the Bible was out again in English available for anybody to read. Cromwell wished for even more copies, fully nine thousand to cover all the parishes in England, and he encouraged daily readings through orders issued by the justices of the peace to set local watches over recalcitrant parish priests.

Rogers had improved the text, other than Tyndale's, as much as he was able, having his own Greek and Latin. Where he had to depend on Miles Coverdale's translation for the other twenty-two books of the Old Testament, he corrected what he could, particularly in the opening chapters of Job. For he too had harbored the lost hope so many then nursed: That if only Tyndale had been spared and not endured Phillips's treachery, if his arrest had been delayed a few more months until the king had come to his present state of mind—perhaps even welcomed Tyndale's return home— then the English Bible might have had the masterwork of an incomparable base text for the Song of Solomon, Job, the Isaiahs, Jeremiah, Ezekiel, and all the other Hebrew poetry that Tyndale had proven he could render.

But at that moment, his very name could never be mentioned. That is why the dedication to Henry VIII had to end: "Your grace's faithful and true subject Thomas Matthews." The supposed name of the author of Matthew's Bible was put together using the Christian names of two saints, because the true author had already been burned as a heretic and must forever remain burned as a heretic. The printers could sneak his initials into the illuminations of the text, as Matthew Crom did with a series of elaborate colophons. They began with IR for John Rogers, HR for Henricus Rex, and RG and ED for Richard Grafton and

Matthew Bible spine. Courtesy of Joe and Jeanne Groberg Collection, on loan to Special collections, Brigham Young University–Idaho Library. Kimball Ungerman, photographer.

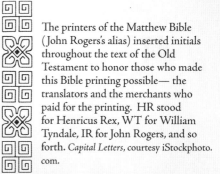

The printers of the Matthew Bible (John Rogers's alias) inserted initials throughout the text of the Old Testament to honor those who made this Bible printing possible— the translators and the merchants who paid for the printing. HR stood for Henricus Rex, WT for William Tyndale, IR for John Rogers, and so forth. *Capital Letters*, courtesy iStockphoto. com.

Edward Whitchurch, those two reforming merchants who had backed Matthew's Bible. Lastly, between the Prophets and the Apocrypha, there is WT. Those initials are the only visible reference to William Tyndale in Matthew's Bible, intended as a monument to his speaking the Word of God surreptitiously to the powers that be.

There is one other distinctive feature to Matthew's Bible—its own unique frontispiece. It does not, for once, illustrate the hierarchy of temporal power in relation to ecclesiastical forces throughout the firmament. No earthly monarch is seated in full figure to dispute spheres of influence with Nobodaddy (a derisive term for the God of Christianity). The entire scene is solely, expansively Paradise Before the Fall (taken from a woodcut in a 1533 Dutch Bible), and the two central figures are Adam and Eve, naked and unabashed. They are clearly in a state of wonderment over so many birds and beasts, the sheer plenty of their surroundings midst hill and dale and pond. The Creator is present up in the cloud tops, but only as a more-or-less distant onlooker. Eve is much more interested in the antics of a pair of monkeys in the opposite treetops. And there is no heavy imagery: No tree of life standing in for the cross, no tempting apple hanging down for Eve to pluck and offer half-eaten to Adam—in fact, no serpent present anywhere on the lush and verdant premises. Adam and Eve are having a nice California day, with the sun in the morning corner and the moon at the other night corner. Nothing could be more delightful, nor of greater primeval innocence.

Too bad, and a great sorrow, that life didn't turn out that way for John Rogers, the maker of Matthew's Bible. He pastored his content German flock until Edward VI came to the throne at the death of King Henry VIII in 1547. Edward was the only son of Henry VIII by his third wife, Jane Seymour, who had died herself at his birth. The child king became the successor, as indicated in a reformist painting by an unknown artist, depicting Henry pointing from his own deathbed to his ten-year-old heir. Edward survived six years after becoming king, dying himself after a sickly and inconsequential reign.

But Rogers returned to London to live in the home of Edward Whitchurch,

"Thomas Matthew's Bible," assembled by John Rogers out of all Tyndale's translations, was printed at Antwerp in 1537, with this frontispiece illustrating a pre-lapsarian Paradise, crowded with forest creatures, even monkeys and merriment. Adam and Eve are shown naked and innocent, while God looks down from above, yet discreetly afar. There is no serpent, not even an apple. Reproduction by kind permission of The Green Collection, Oklahoma City, Oklahoma.

King Henry VIII with his son, King Edward VI, and his third wife, Jane Seymour. Courtesy of The Bridgeman Art Library.

one-half of his publishing team, and to translate works by his Wittenberg mentor Melanchthon. He advanced to various places of residence in London until he arrived at St. Paul's Cathedral as lecturer in divinity, speaking out roundly against the Catholic Duke of Northumberland's misuse of abbey lands. Princess Elizabeth was in his congregation, and he was much respected among reformist churchmen. By 1552, both his wife and their German children had been naturalized as English subjects.

But that very next year, Queen Mary, the Catholic daughter of Henry's divorced first wife, Catherine of Aragon, was brought to the throne as a result of Edward's death. Rogers was placed under house arrest, illegally, then sent to Newgate Prison in 1554, where he was put on trial for heresy on January 27, 1555. He defended himself ably, but was convicted seven days later and was degraded from the priesthood on February 4 in hasty preparation for burning by Queen Mary's London bishop, Stephen Gardiner.

Foxe tells the detailed story, portraying a martyrdom that was far worse than Tyndale's own. Rogers asked if he might speak a few words to his wife before his death—she had been without means of support since his arrest—but he was refused. He was led off to Smithfield and the stake, intoning the psalm *Miserere*. To strengthen his resolve, his wife was there with their eleven children—one, whom he had never before seen, at her breast. At the stake, he was offered a pardon, should he recant, but he firmly refused and exhorted the people to stand firm in the faith he had taught them.

Catholic clergy with Queen Mary at court. Courtesy of The Bridgeman Art Library.

Foxe reports that when the fire reached him, "he, as one feeling no smart, washed his hands in the flame, as though it had been in cold water." He then lifted his hands to heaven and did not move them again until they were consumed in the devouring fire.

John Rogers was the first of some three hundred martyrs burned at the stake by Bloody Queen Mary during her five-year reign.

chapter

7

THE GREAT BIBLE vs. THE GENEVA BIBLE vs. THE BISHOPS' BIBLE

We are getting ahead of ourselves here historically, rushing through a time when Henry VIII indicated royal favor toward allowing an English Bible in the Church, increasingly considered his to command. To a surprising extent, the growing distribution of these several English Bibles printed abroad had begun to have favorable effect on the people's literacy at home, right down to the plowboy. In fact, there was soon a dearth of Matthew's Bibles available from that short run of fifteen hundred. Cromwell, with Archbishop Cranmer's encouragement, decided to alleviate the shortage by launching a revision of Matthew's Bible in a larger folio format that would make the Good Book a dominant presence in every parish church. It came to be called the Great Bible, which it surely was by virtue of its sharply increased page size.

Coverdale's 1535 Bible measured roughly 11 inches by 7 inches, and Matthew's Bible swelled to 12 inches by 9 inches; the Great Bible stood 2 inches taller at 14 inches high and 9 inches wide. It was also to be an authorized edition of the Holy Bible in English—the only such sacred text up to, and including, the KJV (which, despite a common misunderstanding, was never authorized by King James). Only King

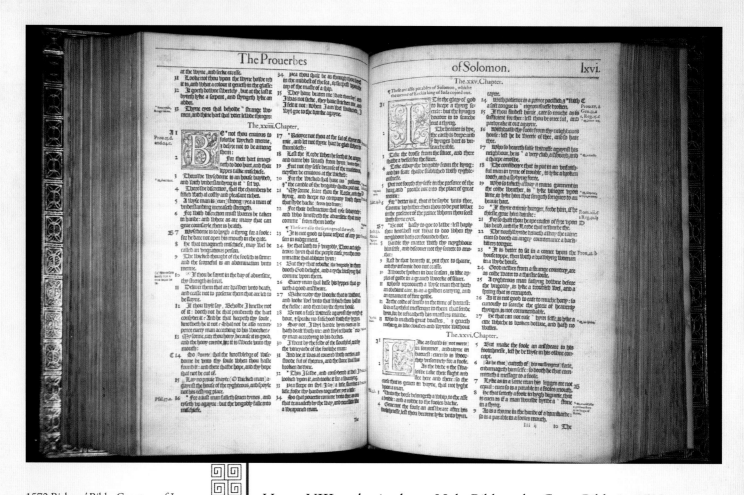

Henry VIII authorized any Holy Bible—the Great Bible in 1539, as a strong indication of his early support.

The editing and revisions of the Great Bible were assigned to Miles Coverdale, a politic choice. Two-thirds of the projected Great Bible was already Tyndale's translation of the New Testament and his completed books of the Old Testament. But Coverdale's capabilities as a Latinist would avail him of sufficient latitude to "tweak" the text to calm the concerns of the more severe clerics who considered Greek and Hebrew scholars subversive interlopers upon their received Vulgate text. Coverdale would prove helpful in favoring the Latin versions of the Old Testament prophets whom Tyndale hadn't translated, and his smoothly flowing English, so musical in his psalms, could be depended on to echo well from the stone chancels of their Gothic churches.

The decision was also made to do the printing in Paris at the presses of François Regnault. This was proposed for greater elegance, since the French were far more advanced in the book trade than any English print shop. But it brought grave consequences when conservative English bishops conspired with the French court to halt the printing altogether. Coverdale wrote in a panic that twenty-five hundred copies had been seized for burning by the Inquisition. Grafton, the London publisher, and Whitchurch reported, "Not only the same bibles being XXV in number were seized and made confiscate, but also the printer, merchants and correctors with great jeopardy of their lives escaped."

The confiscation was done according to instructions the pope issued on December 24, 1538, to one of his representatives in Scotland, but the bitter disagreement became even more complicated when a French privateer named Pierre Beaufort captured the German merchant ship *George*. Beaufort killed the wounded and set the five remaining German crew adrift. Then Beaufort himself was taken with his prize by the English, and both were brought into harbor at Whitby. Beaufort escaped to Scotland and sued for return of his prize, while the surviving *George* crew miraculously drifted to English shores to tell tales of their savage treatment by the French. Beaufort was arrested but still laid claim to the *George* before Thomas Howard, Duke of Norfolk, also the Lord Admiral of England and an implacable Catholic foe of Thomas Cromwell. Cromwell appointed a Westminster commission of lawyer-bishops who not only denied Beaufort's recovery of his prize but found that the captured goods must revert to their German consigners. The Duke of Norfolk felt humiliated, as did all of Catholic France.

How did this unforeseen event get so involved in the printing of the Great Bible?

"Immediately on the seizure of the sheets in Paris and the flight of the English team, Cromwell met with Castillon [the French ambassador in London]," writes Professor A. J. Slavin regarding this misadventure. "He thoroughly briefed the ambassador on the Bible project, mentioning his own investment of 600 marks in the undertaking while broadly hinting that immediate delivery of the sheets might ease the way toward a settlement of other matters then at issue between England and France."

So it looked as if the times were ripe for quietly exchanging the captured *George* for the twenty-five hundred sets of unbound copies still in Paris under the care of the Inquisitor General. In April 1539, another printing of the Great Bible was done in London at the Grey Friars; well under Cromwell's control, that printing produced three thousand copies, mixing Paris and London pages, though none were sold until November. The cross-dealings with the French were touchy and intricate, but with the freed copies at last shipped from France and a second printing of three thousand more at the Grey Friars a year later, the parish pulpits were at last being supplied with the Great Bible by 1539. In triumph, Cromwell was elevated to the peerage as the Earl of Essex.

But the newly acclaimed earl was already beginning to lose his grip on power at the hands of the vengeful Duke of Norfolk and the conservative bishops acting through Parliament. They passed the Act of Uniformity of Opinion, along with the Six Articles, restoring all the clerical practices that Tyndale had so stubbornly fought as a reforming Puritan: masses for the dead, the fabrication of "Purgatory," and the Church's seven sacraments instead of the New Testament's two—holy baptism and the Eucharist. The Six Articles reestablished—on pain of death—transubstantiation (the changing of the bread and water into the flesh and blood of Christ), compulsory confession to the priest's ear (listening in for God), restricted

Psalms of David with music score. Courtesy of Harold B. Lee Special Collections, BYU Library. Kimball Ungerman, photographer.

The Great Bible. Courtesy of Joe and Jeanne Groberg Collection, on loan to Special Collections, Brigham Young University–Idaho Library. Kimball Ungerman, photographer.

Title page of the Great Bible, possibly from King Henry VIII's own personal Bible. Reproduced by permission of The British Library.

communion for the majority of religious worshippers, inviolability of monastic vows, private masses, and, above all, celibate priests.

Tyndale had been especially outspoken in favor of married clergy. "He must have a wife for two causes. One, that it may thereby be known who is meet for the room. He is unapt for so chargeable an office, which never had a household to rule. Another is that chastity is an exceeding seldom gift, and unchastity exceeding perilous . . . inasmuch as the people look as well unto the living as unto the preaching, and are hurt at once if the living disagree, and fall from the faith, and believe not the word." It scores a telling point that the early readers of Tyndale's New Testament were shocked to discover that Jesus' disciples were married. And there is surely a lesson to be taken to heart from the abnormal course followed by Henry VIII, as once the Defender of the Faith, in his own repeated forays into misalliance.

On June 10, 1540—only weeks after the Great Bibles first reached their churches—Cromwell was arrested at the Council Table for heresy and treason. He had led Henry VIII miserably into his unwanted fourth marriage to Anne of Cleves, and he had failed to gain French backing against the pope, who had pronounced the excommunication of King Henry VIII. The new lady occupying the King's royal attention was Catherine Howard, niece of the Duke of Norfolk. The Earl of Essex was undone, charged with corruption in conspiring against the French claims for Beaufort's letter of marque in order to convert part of the prize to his own use. He railed against these charges in a letter on July 24, answering that the Duke of Norfolk and three bishops— including Cuthburt Tunstall—knew it wasn't true. But what they still claimed to know was that Cromwell must have turned the French prize to "his own use" in negotiating with the French for those sheets of this authorized but heretical English Bible to be placed in every church in England.

Cromwell was executed, without trial, four days later.

Yet the Great Bible stood open at last on the pulpits, with its title page prominently proclaiming across its central panel: "The Bible in English." The surrounding illustrations on that same title page, however, thoroughly depict what remained the true state of affairs across all of England. Gone is any naked Paradise from the former Matthew's Bible. Here instead is a crowded royal audience, with King Henry VIII seated prominently topside, by far the grandest figure, aloft on his throne. He is shown handing off the *Verbum Dei*—the constitution on divine revelation— to Archbishop Cranmer on his right side and to ex-Vice-Regent Cromwell on his left. Below the king, these two high-ranking members of the clergy appear again, wearing their proper headdresses and handing off smaller packets of the *Verbum Dei* to a priest and a nobleman. Finally, at the bottom of this page we see the lower classes, an over-dressed but nondescript crowd. None of them is reading from any Bible in English, nor holding anything in his or her hands whatsoever; from above, the crowd is being harangued by a priest, in Latin, forewarning them that "supplications, prayers, intercessions, and giving of thanks" must be made "for kings, and for all that are in authority." The only words these people are shown to answer in return are *Vivat Rex* ("Long live the king!")—repeatedly, in tag after tag, in Latin, not English. If the crowds fail to answer properly, there in the far bottom right corner is Newgate Prison, where several such quelled dissenters are already behind bars.

This visual message that introduces the first "authorized" English Bible—which this very churched volume chained to the pulpit surely is—delivered a hierarchical assault on any reformation affecting the

The first reading of the English Bible, English School, twentieth century. Private Collection, © Look and Learn, the Bridgeman Art Library.

English people. After Cromwell's execution in 1540, his coat-of-arms was removed from the title page of the fourth edition, not unlike the name of a condemned Soviet member of the Politburo being removed from atop Lenin's tomb. He survived anonymously only as a circular white space, defacing his coat of arms.

In contrast, the reaction of the English commoners to these handsome English Bibles was ecstatic, then increasingly disorderly. Such beautiful books were supposed to be read quietly "without disputation," but Puritan readers read out loud inside the churches, then louder and louder, and fell to arguing over interpretation. The Church began to issue and post formal "Admonitions" that set rules for reading scripture. But dissenting congregants ignored them, deliberately raising their voices to disrupt the services at the altar, reading and disputing from under the very Admonition posted above the Great Bible. Everybody was reading the Good Book, or having it read to them, in a highly fluent and talkative burst of spiritual freedom, as they did in the primitive church (see Col. 4:16).

This first spread social uneasiness, then the sharp threat of persecution. Hugh Latimer, a popular churchman made bishop of Worcester in 1535, resigned his watch over the Six Articles. He was imprisoned by Henry VIII but released in 1547 by Edward VI, whose brief reign set a renewed but uncertain reforming trend. Indeed, the notable service of Katherine Parr, Henry's last wife and surviving widow, was to sustain the teenaged Edward in his devotion to the Protestant cause.

Latimer preached a famous sermon the next year entitled *On the Plough* that compared plowing to preaching, the labor and duty of all bishops: "scripture calleth it meat; not strawberries, that come but once a year, and tarry not long, but are soon gone." Once again, someone holy was speaking up for the ploughboy, but on her ascension to the throne, the Catholic Queen Mary had Latimer arrested again and convicted of heresy.

More was disturbed by the writings of William Tyndale and ordered him hunted down and arrested.

"You could argue that Henry VIII's Reformation didn't stay the course. It petered out. His son Edward followed on, kept the Church of England going, but when Edward died, and Mary took over, there was a change. It was back to the Catholic Church. She didn't want to be head of the Church of England. She was after all the daughter of Catherine of Aragon, a very good member of the Catholic Church."

—Lucy Worsley
Chief Curator, Historic Royal Palaces, London, England

A Table describing the burning of B. Ridley, and Father Latimer at Oxford, D. Smith there preaching at the time of their Martyrdome.

On October 16, 1555, Latimer and Nicholas Ridley, another dissenting churchman, were burned outside Balliol College at Oxford. "Be of good cheer, master Riley, and play the man," Latimer cried. "We shall this day light such a candle, by God's grace, in England, as I trust shall never be put out."

At this same spot outside Balliol College, another famous martyr—the deposed Archbishop Thomas Cranmer—was burned.

Queen Mary imprisoned Thomas Cranmer and, using inquisitors, extracted many a confession from him, each more guilt ridden than the last. But he was still sentenced to death, and on the day of execution in 1556, he was given one final chance to make a public recantation.

October 16, 1555, Hugh Latimer was burned at the stake under the decree of Queen Mary. Courtesy of Foxe's *Book of Martyrs*.

"Cranmer had been promoted to Archbishop for his loyal service as Anne Boleyn's chaplain. He was instrumental in facilitating Henry's divorce from Catherine of Aragon and personally crowned Anne Boleyn queen, a fact that Mary would not forget nor forgive. But what he is best known for today by Christians, members of the Church of England, is for putting together the structures of the Church of England, things like the Thirty-Nine Articles, the Book of Common Prayer."

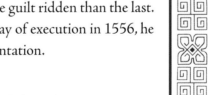

—Lucy Worsley
Chief Curator, Historic Royal Palaces, London, England

The B O O K of
Common Prayer,
And Adminiftration of the
SACRAMENTS,
AND OTHER
RITES and CEREMONIES
OF THE
C H U R C H,
According to the Ufe of
The CHURCH of ENGLAND:
TOGETHER WITH THE
P S A L T E R
OR
PSALMS of DAVID,
Pointed as they are to be fung or faid in Churches.

C A M B R I D G E,
Printed by JOHN BASKERVILLE, Printer to the Univerfity;
by whom they are fold, and by B. DOD, Bookfeller,
in Ave-Mary Lane, London. M DCC LXI.
(Price Eight Shillings and Six Pence, unbound.)

The Book of Common Prayer

"You can see the English Bible as the absolute bedrock of the English Reformation. But alongside that was a special book for England, a new way of worshiping, the *Book of Common Prayer*. And the great thing about that book was that it was in English for the first time when all the services of the Church had been in Latin before. So this was s book very explicitly intended to be 'understanded of people,' as the phrase was at the time.

"*The Book of Common Prayer* was a performative text that was recited by virtually every English citizen every week for centuries during their Sunday worship. It suffused their lives with Cranmer's version of the English language and along with the English Bible defined that English language. Shakespeare's language is important, hugely important, but it is the Bible, first, *Book of Common Prayer*, second, and Shakespeare, third."

—Diarmaid MacCulloch
Professor DM, University of Oxford, England

The Book of Common Prayer printed by John Baskerville, 1762. Courtesy Wikimedia Commons.

"And as he went to the stake, he was supposed to announce his recantation of Protestant beliefs but instead he held out his right hand in the fire and said, 'This is the hand I signed the recantations with and this will burn first.' And he died affirming, in fact, his Protestant confession."

—Susannah Monta
Professor of English; University of Notre Dame, Indiana

That bright candle lit before Balliol flared proverbially for all the reforming clergy who then fled England, yet again abroad—this time largely into the Academy of Geneva that had become the Reformation's central institution for advanced biblical scholarship and promulgation of Protestant theology. John Calvin as its chief Latinist was joined by Theodore Beza, a renowned Greek scholar, to set the tone. An improvement over the more desperate circumstances of earlier Antwerp, the well-established Academy of Geneva first printed Pierre Robert Olivétan's French New Testament, then Olivétan's "noble folio Bible," which actually had influenced John Rogers's work in Antwerp on his Matthew's Bible.

Among the English exiles to Geneva was a printer, Rowland Hall, formerly of the Stationers' Company in London, who set up his own English press. The "learned men"—who gathered around the academy to "peruse" the existing English versions of the New Testament—included Oxbridge reformers like Hebrew scholar Anthony Gilbey, Thomas Sampson, William Williams, Christopher Goodman, John Barton, Thomas Cole, Thomas Wood, and William Kethe. The group also included reformers we already know, including John Bale, John Knox, John Bodley, John Foxe, and even Miles Coverdale. It seems William Wittingham—a Greek scholar, fellow of All Souls, and later Dean of Christ Church—turned his pen to the New Testament, again closely following Tyndale. His translation was published by Hall in 1557.

Its printing followed the more readable French format of Olivétan, which featured numbered verses in attractive Roman type, abandoning the long paragraphs in black letter printing. Paragraphs were previously indicated only by paragraph marks in the margins. For the first time, English scripture had an open, modernized ease along with precise textual improvements. Consider Jesus' short parable in Luke 15:8–10. Here is Tyndale's version in 1534:

> Either what woman having ten groats, if she lose one, doth not light a candle, and sweep the house, and seek diligently till she find it? And when she hath found it, she calleth her lovers and her neighbours saying: Rejoice with me, for I had found the groat which I had lost. Likewise I say unto you, joy is made in the presence of the angels of God over one sinner that repenteth.

John Calvin, 1509–1564. Courtesy Wikimedia.

Burning of Thomas Cranmer, Archbishop of Canterbury, was executed on March 21, 1556, under Queen Mary I. He recanted Protestantism while in prison, but recanted his recantation just before he died. Courtesy Foxe's *Book of Martyrs*.

The description of D. Cranmer, how he was plucked down from the stage, by Friars and Papists, for the true Confession of his faith.

The burning of D. Thomas Cranmer, Archbishop of Canterbury, in the Town ditch at Oxford, with his hand first thrust into the fire, where he subscribed be

Contrast that with this version from 1557:

8. Either what woman having ten pieces of silver, if she lose one, doth not light a candle, and sweep the room, and seek diligently till she find it?

9. And when she hath found it, she calleth her friends and her neighbors saying: Rejoice with me, for I have found the piece which I had lost.

10. Likewise I say unto you, joy is made in the presence of the Angels of God, over the one sinner that converteth.

The steps through the three verses are swift and logical, and the updates—"ten pieces of silver" instead of "groats," "friends" instead of "lovers"—are accommodating, and the KJV retained both of them. But KJV returned to "sinner that repenteth," keeping the stronger Tyndale, while avoiding at all costs the Catholic Rheims' only requirement for a "sinner that do repentance."

The same "learned men" started a few months later on another complete English Bible, using the same format of verses and lightened Roman typefaces. It was well illustrated, and five pages of maps were also provided with views of the Holy Land, right down to the location where Moses led the Israelite crossing of the Red Sea.

Queen Mary died on November 18, 1558, and many Protestant exiles, some eight hundred altogether on the continent, returned to welcome the Anglican Good Queen Bess. But a crew stayed behind in Switzerland "for the space of two years and more day and night" to bring about the first English Geneva Bible in April 1560. They included Anthony Gilby, Christopher Goodman, William Cole, and Thomas Sampson, but they were probably led once more by William Wittingham. The printing, done again by Rowland Hall, was financed by John Bodley, the wealthy London merchant whose son Thomas founded the Bodleian Library at Oxford.

The Geneva Version immediately became the Bible of the English people and especially of the Scots—then, via the KJV, it eventually became the Bible of all English-speaking people everywhere, as Winston Churchill would have us be. If the Great Bible lay heavily upon the pulpit, the Geneva Bible was taken up to be read comfortably at home.

One of the Geneva Bible's claims to fame—which so bothered King James—is

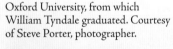

Oxford University, from which William Tyndale graduated. Courtesy of Steve Porter, photographer.

Geneva Bible quarto. Courtesy of Joe and Jeanne Groberg Collection, on loan to Special Collections, Brigham Young University–Idaho Library. Kimball Ungerman, photographer.

its 250 marginal notes. Critics argued that they were too proselytizing, but out of all of them, John Eadie neutrally finds that "not more than ten of them are unmistakably Calvinistic utterances." The rest were either factually neutral or hierarchically—not doctrinally—offensive. Above all, the notes helped any early English reader overcome his likely ignorance of required biblical history.

The arrival of the Geneva Bible on English shores has been called "the first great achievement of Elizabeth's reign," and it was renewed in one edition every year until 1616. Though licensed in England, it was never actually printed in England until 1576. After 1616, it was prohibited, probably because it created unwanted competition for the KJV. Still, the Dutch continued printing the Geneva Bible abroad through 1644, distributing 150,000 more copies. And the Geneva Bible's far passage to the American continent with the Pilgrims—if less so with the Puritans, who were more inclined to the KJV—was another religious triumph. For the first time, the English Old Testament reflected the poetry of its entire Hebrew base text, as Tyndale had tried to do originally.

One way to glimpse the majesty of the Geneva Version is to read closely into the verses of Second Isaiah, chapter 40. The last time these verses had been attempted in English was by Coverdale for the revised Great Bible, culled from secondary sources and done in long paragraphs. But here, these verses are separated out, again by the numbers, so that the

poetry, translated directly from the Hebrew, is first visible, then audible in the parallel English tones.

> Comfort ye, comfort ye my people, will your God say.
>
> Speak ye comfortably to Jerusalem, and cry unto her, that her welfare is accomplished, that her iniquity is pardoned: for she hath received of the Lord's hand double of her sins.
>
> A voice crieth in the wilderness, Prepare ye the way of the Lord: make straight in the desert a path for our God.
>
> Every valley shall be exalted, and every mountain and hill shall be made low: and the crooked shall be made straight, and the rough places plain.
>
> And the glory of the Lord shall be revealed, and all flesh shall see it together: for the mouth of the Lord hath spoken it.
>
> A voice said, Cry. And he said, What shall I cry? All flesh is grass, and all the grass thereof is the flower of the field.
>
> The grass withereth, the flower fadeth. Because the Spirit of the Lord bloweth upon it: surely the people is grass.
>
> The grass withereth, the flower fadeth: but the word of our God shall stand for ever.

And so forth. . .

In the marginal notes to the Geneva Bible, attention is called to "Comfort ye" as assurance that "they shall never be destitute of Prophets . . . to assure them of their deliverance of body and soul." Then "Prepare ye the way" is glossed, historically: "Meaning Cyrus and Darius which should deliver God's people out of captivity, and make them a ready way to Jerusalem: and this was fully accomplished when John the Baptist brought tidings of Jesus Christ's coming who was the true deliverer of his Church from sin and Satan, Matthew 3.3." But this "voice crying in the wilderness"—a most frequent KJV quotation—is better translated, say more modern speakers of Hebrew, as "the way" in "the wilderness," so that today's ARV reads: "The voice of one that crieth, Prepare ye the wilderness way." The most recent version is less poetic, but proof of how constantly revision is required.

Later, "All flesh shall see it together" is glossed, "This miracle shall be so great, that it shall be known through all the world." References to "the flesh is grass" and "the people are grass" actually strike me as a premonition of how Walt Whitman came to seize on the imagery of *Leaves of Grass*, and quite suit the fair warning that "Even the young men shall faint," for such are "They that trust in their own virtue and do not acknowledge that all cometh of God."

Finally there is Daniell's astute observation that "the crooked shall be straight and the rough places plain" along that wilderness path to Jerusalem was adroitly caught by the librettist Charles Jennens for Handel's *Messiah*, even as these very words were being taken up by the KJV. That represents the remarkable flowing together of the cultural Christian faith in the eighteenth century, despite the impact of Deism during this prevalent Age of Reason.

The influence of the Geneva Bible has been enormous, despite its later disappearance, and some critics argue that it should rightfully enjoy a greater historical prominence beside its rival KJV. It glories directly in the supreme sovereignty of God through the Word of God (*Sola Scrypta*). It once spoke to our greatest writers, Spenser and Shakespeare and Milton, and other Elizabethan and Jacobean poets, and carried forward the beacon of liberty throughout the seventeenth century. If its clarifying marginal notes, along with its apparatus and format, could be adopted by some editions of the KJV, why wasn't everything made whole by transferring its passionate text, since so many parts were already familiar to English readers, in one body of belief?

Whenever any such threatening cries arose from reforming quarters, the established church hierarchy edged forth with an embracing proposal for yet another, better, more uniform, slightly larger, though necessarily English Bible. If the Great Bible was not winning the hearts—let alone the minds—of the people, why not try again with an error-free book written in common, everyday language to be released through the church to those deemed far more worthy readers than the Puritan dissenters?

That is exactly what Matthew Parker—newly appointed Archbishop of Canterbury by Elizabeth I in 1559—proposed: An English Bible to be done by the bishops themselves. He too had once been Anne Boleyn's chaplain, so he surely knew of Tyndale's work. He approved of the Geneva Bible, at least for reading at home, since Queen Elizabeth had granted John Bodley an exclusive patent to distribute the Geneva Version for seven years in England. He surely understood his queen's preference for Protestantism, the so-called Elizabethan Establishment. But Parker had judiciously gone all the way back to Thomas Cranmer's 1533 proposal to publish a Bishops' Bible. Archbishop Parker reproposed this to William

Matthew Parker, 1504–1575, Archbishop of Canterbury for sixteen years. Courtesy Wikimedia.

PARKERUS *docuit praesul, dein docta reliquit Scripta, et Scriptores eruit è tenebris.*
b b.

63

Cecil, Queen Elizabeth's secretary, since "god be praised, ye have men able to do it thoroughly." They should produce a revision that was structurally orthodox, that would be acceptable to the conservative authorities who still governed the Church of England.

In addition, Parker asked that "in jug only have the preferment of this version." That is, he asked that the London printer Richard Jugge be granted a monopoly on the sale of the Bishops' Bible "for if any other should lurch him to steal from him his [copyrights], he were a great loser in his first doing"—in other words, his initial capital investment. In truth, Parker's only real, if ulterior, purpose seems to have been to drive out the Geneva Bible from its more general circulation. The bishops came through with their texts in remarkably short order, after somewhat indiscriminate assignment, and Jugge printed a handsome folio, another inch taller than the Great Bible. Indeed, there is no richer, more sumptuous English Bible from the sixteenth century than the Bishops' Bible, published in 1568. It was reprinted a dozen times by Jugge before his death in 1577, twenty more times before 1611, and four more times thereafter. Though it was beautiful in appearance, by general agreement it was the worst translation ever, bordering on utterly detestable.

When the Archbishop sent a bound copy to Queen Elizabeth with her gentle portrait on the title page, asking that she license it to be the only Bible for public reading in the churches, "to draw to one uniformity," she refused. It might have been her will to remain regally neutral on many questions of religious choice, since she calculated on support from all her realm's people, but it could also have been that, as a right speaker of English herself and even a theatre-goer familiar with Shakespeare, she quickly glanced at the Bishops' rendering of the 23rd Psalm: "God is my shepherd, therefore I can lack nothing: He will cause me to repose myself in pasture full of grass, and he will lead me unto calm waters."

As Professor Gerald Hammond, literary and Hebrew scholar, proclaims: "Words and more words is the great belief of this translator, born, no doubt, out of his belief in what constitutes good English style." Of the entire enterprise, he concludes: "For the most part the Bishops' Bible is either a lazy and ill-informed collection of what had been done before, or, in its original parts, the work of third-rate scholars and second-rate writers. In no way could it hold comparison with the Geneva Bible."

That the practicing Anglican clergy understood this imposition of the Bishops' Bible to be wrong-headed themselves is clear from a study of their continued use of the Geneva Bible in their own sermons. Over the next fifty years, it was still in second place on Anglican lecterns, despite Parker's forced sales of the Bishops' Bible. Even more damning, a study of some fifty sermons by bishops from 1611 to 1630—including those of Lancelot Andrewes, the chief KJV reviser, and William Laud, who stood opposed to all things evangelical—reveals them taking their texts from the Geneva Bible twenty-seven times, while taking their texts from the Bishops'

Elizabeth frontispiece in the Bishops' Bible. Courtesy Wikimedia.

Bible in only five instances. Among the twenty or so remaining sermonizers, only half picked up their text from the then-recent KJV, made all the more significant since after 1616 the Geneva Bible was banned from England.

This spells out in ecclesiastical behavior what the Anglican bishops had decided about their own Bishops' Bible. As bookman A. W. Pollard argues, "to the very end of his life Parker used his control over the Stationers' Company to prevent the Geneva version being printed in England."

"It seems certain that the Archbishop cared little for providing Bibles for private reading," Pollard continues. "He saw and met the need of suitable service for the church, but . . . he did not 'trust the people' with cheap editions of the Bible, and his lack of confidence sealed the fate of the Bishops' Bible."

The final irony is that in 1605 King James gave each member of his revising panels the second (1572) edition of the Bishops' Bible as their base text for their grand effort to create the KJV.

The chief advisor to the six companies of KJV translators was Lancelot Andrewes. Courtesy of The Bridgeman Art Library.

chapter

8

THE RHEIMS NEW TESTAMENT, 1582

The Catholic Church translated the Bible into English at the Rheims monastery. Named the Douay-Rheims Bible, it allowed church members to also hear the words of the Bible in a more common tongue.

The only remaining English translation not yet discussed before English scholars gathered to create the KJV was created through Catholic authorship during Elizabeth's reign, a translation done at the English Roman Catholic College across the Channel in Rheims, France. The college was part of the University of Douai established by Phillip II of Spain in 1562, to which the institution later returned to take up the translation of an English Catholic Bible in 1610. But the immediate task begun in 1578 was the Rheims New Testament, a translation sorely needed among English Catholics who faced rival Protestant English Bibles in common hands on all sides of sectarian contention. Such was previously heresy, according to strict Catholic dogma, but maybe it was time their own celebrants got in on the going thing in Elizabethan England. So the Rheims New Testament stands curiously within the great sixteenth-century tradition of English Bible-making, since it was, even as a translation from the Latin Vulgate, still (supposedly) grounded on the original Greek, which brought on the challenge of Erasmus, with its inevitable codependence on the early English New Testament from the "heretic" William Tyndale.

Thus was the complicated controversy reversed for the Catholic exiles and those who refused to attend the Church of England as they suddenly faced prosecution under Queen Elizabeth's new sovereignty: now they were obliged to produce Catholic scripture in the English language overseas for their English flock. They were also forced to pamphleteer secretly for their own religious causes out of their "priest holes," such as did Robert Parsons, William Allen, Henry Garnett, Edmund Campion, and Robert Southwell. Despite their reluctance to leave their Church Latin behind, they found they would have to move closer to the Protestant ascendency in biblical oratory through their command of common English.

Gregory Martin began his translation of the Rheims New Testament on or about March 16, 1578. He wrote two English chapters per day—keyed to the Latin Vulgate, which he held to be "truer than the vulgar Greek itself." His work was checked carefully by William Allen (later Cardinal) as president of the college, and scholars Richard Bristow and William Reynolds; all were originally friends from the college. Cardinal Allen had been promised by Pope Sixtus V the honor of reconciling England to the papacy when and if the Spanish Armada should emerge victorious, but pleas for acceptance of the Rheims New Testament depended far more on Martin's excuses that the "[Holy Church or the governors] have neither of old nor of late, ever wholly condemned all vulgar versions of Scriptures, nor have generally forbidden the faithful to read the same." Really?

Yes, truly, denies Martin against all the evidence, but likewise never imagine, he says, "that our forefathers suffered every school-master, scholar, or grammarian that had a little Greek or Latin, straight to take in hand the holy Testament: or that the translated Bible into the vulgar tongues were in the hands of every husbandman, artificer, prentice, boys, girls, mistress, maid, [and] man: that they were for table talk, for ale benches, for boats and barges, and for every profane person and company. No, in these better

Rheims Bible compared with Bishops' Bible; comparison done by William Fulke. Courtesy of Joe and Jeanne Groberg Collection, on loan to Special Collections, Brigham Young University–Idaho Library. Kimball Ungerman, photographer.

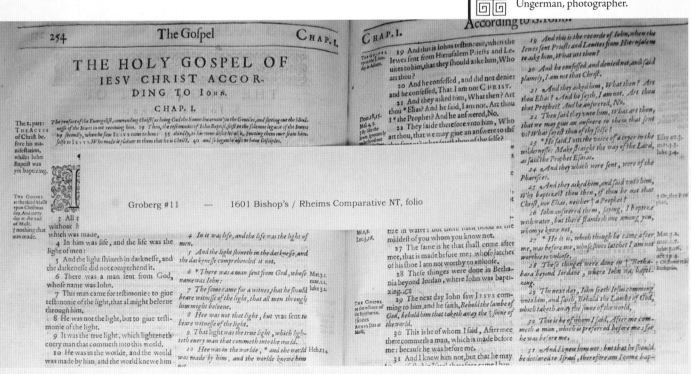

For more than a hundred years, it was unlawful to possess an English-language Bible in England.

Closeup of Latin Vulgate Bible page. Courtesy of Harold B. Lee Special Collections, BYU Library. Kimball Ungerman, photographer.

times men were neither so ill, nor so curious of themselves, so as to abuse the blessed book of Christ: neither was there any such easy means before printing was invented, to disperse the copies into the hands of every man, as there is now."

Yea, pray remember: "The poor ploughman, could then in labouring the ground, could sing the hymns and psalms whether in known or unknown languages, as they heard them in the holy Church, though they could neither read nor know the sense, meanings and mysteries of the Same."

Altogether, Martin offers ten good reasons why he dared to claim, "We translate the old Latin text, not the common Greek text." One of them was that the Latin Vulgate "followeth the Greek more exactly than the Protestant's translation." Often he indeed does pursue the Latin so scrupulously that it sounds like all Greek to his readers—Ephesians 3:6, "concorporat and comparticipant," or 2 Peter 2:13, "conquinations, following on spots and delicacies," and other perplexing phrases. But on other occasions, why is Martin so dependent on obvious borrowings from earlier Protestant texts—Tyndale or Coverdale or even the Geneva Bible itself? Once again, Tyndale's epic rendering of the prodigal son from 1526 stands out (however flawed) as 80 percent of Martin's version:

And he said, a certain man had two sons: and the younger of them said to his father, Father, give me the portion of the substance that belongeth to me. And he divided unto them the substance. And not many days after the younger son gathering all his things together went from home into a far country: and there he wasted his substance living riotously.

Here, according to Daniell's exceedingly close analysis, "portion" came from the Geneva; the first "substance" came from Tyndale, Geneva, and KJV;

and "goods" is from the Latin *substantia*, used by Martin here three times for the two distinct Greek words *ousia* (substance, property) for the son's things and *bios* (living, livelihood) for what the father gives. "Not many days" is both the Latin *non post multos dies*, and the Greek *met ou pollas hemeras*, which Tyndale had paraphrased to "not long after," followed by the Great Bible and Geneva; KJV followed the Latin, "not many days." Martin is alone in "all his things" (Latin, *omnibus*), where Tyndale's more thorough "all that he had" from the Greek intensive of "everything" (*hapanta*) went forward with Great and Geneva, weakened by KJV to "all." Martin is also alone in "went from home" rather than Tyndale's "took his journey" (Great, Geneva, and KJV); there the one Greek word (*apedemesen*) communicates the sense of going abroad; the Latin in three words, *pergere profectus est*, intensifies the sense of travel. Martin's fumbling phrase "went from home" simply does not reach out far enough.

Clerics read William Fulke's comparison of the Rheims Bible and the Bishops' Bible.

Martin ends the parable:

> Son, thou art always with me, and all my things are thine. But it behoved us to make merry and be glad, because this thy brother was dead, and is revived, was lost, and is found.

Another 80 percent of this came from Tyndale, with Martin's awkward changes not going forward to the KJV. The change of "was" to "art" came from Geneva.

The Rheims New Testament (1582) is also petulant in Martin's notes to his cross-ruffing text. As one example, consider Christ's outcry to God as Christ hung on the cross: "Why has thou forsaken me?" (Matt. 27:46). "[B]eware of the detestable blasphemy of Calvin and the Calvinists," writes Martin, "who thinking not the bodily death of Christ sufficient, say, that he was also here forsaken and abandoned by his father [!?]."

Tyndale gives only the prior reference to Psalm 22:1, and the Geneva did the same, adding, with reference to *forsaken*—"To wit, in this misery. And this crying out is proper to his humanity, which not withstanding was void of sin, but yet it felt the wrath of God, which is due to our sins."

Gregory Martin's preface to his Rheims New Testament (1582) is an infamous and lengthy discourse, twenty-six pages of irritable denunciation of Protestant "heresy." His Rheims clearly demanded an answer, since it was too devious to be ignored—constantly maintaining the Greek was corrupt, the Latin definitive—insomuch that William Fulke, master of Pembroke College, Cambridge, issued *A Defence of the Sincere and True Translations of the Holy Scripture into the English Tongue, against G. Martin*. Whereunto is added a brief confutation of Cavils by *Diverse Papists in their English Pamphlets, against the Writings of W. Fulke.*

In his thoroughness, Fulke chose to reprint the Rheims New Testament side by side with the matching text in the Bishops' Bible, so that the reader could ferret out all these papist errors by closely comparing the parallel columns. This made for another handsome folio first printed by Robert Barker in 1589, but it may have also given the Rheims an inadvertent extra boost up in biblical stature for the final face-off inspired by King James's call for a new translation. A team of modern bibliophiles—T. H. Darlow, H. F. Moule, and A. S. Herbert—concludes that this round of the battle over words helped qualify the Rheims Testament for the main joust over the KJV.

Ironically, this counterblast against Martin—printing the Rheims New Testament in full, side by side with the Bishops' version—secured for the Rheims New Testament a wide publicity that it would not otherwise have obtained and was indirectly responsible for the marked influence Rheims exerted on the Bible of 1611.

So in his outspoken orthodoxy, Martin succeeded. As S. L. Greenslade in *The Cambridge History of the Bible* confidently asserts, "If ever a vernacular Bible was combative and tendentious [biased], this was—in its Vulgate basis, the version itself, the marginal notes, the lengthy annotations." Greenslade never even mentions the rowling spurs of Gregory Martin's preface.

chapter
9
THE KING JAMES VERSION

The King James translation began in 1604. Fifty-four scholars, divided into six companies, began this effort, which lasted seven years.

The King James Version was not, of course, done by King James, any more than it was "authorized" by His Majesty—even though he was oft hailed as "a living library and a walking study" whenever he commented on witches, amusements on Sunday, or the removal of supposedly "idolatrous" images from churches. In fact, he had very shrewd reasons for gathering his esteemed clergy together at Hampton Court just after the Christmas season, or "the Hols," as the British now call their annual holly-leafed celebrations.

James's greatest worry came down to what an early Tudor poet warned against: "Thunder rolls round the throne." Anybody who crawled too close to the throne to toy with the ways of the monarchy was very likely to be struck by deadly lightning.

James was exceedingly anxious that such thunder not occur around His throne. So on the first day of the conference, he gave audience solely to the royal clergy, princes of his church, though he was unexpectedly harsh on these bishops. He warned them against their abuses, particularly the practice of one priest holding several benefices and raking in all the money.

Hampton Court

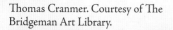

"The conference was held at Hampton Court because that was where the royal court spent Christmas in the winter of 1603, the beginning of 1604. They had to be out of town because of the Plague. And there is a strange irony because the court's Christmas at Hampton Court had been this huge party, celebration, masquing event, and King James was very conscious that kingship is a performance. He wrote himself, 'The king is one who sits on a stage, somebody who will be looked at, respected, judged.' And he and his courtiers had been acting out all sorts of lavish and extraordinary scenes in masques and performances just before the conference got going. And I think this gives us a clue what the conference seemed to the king, himself. He saw it as a performance of his authority. If you look at the way the conference room was set up, he was seated in the prime position . . . an X-framed chair of kingship beneath a canopy of estate in the most important room in the palace. So don't get the idea they were all sitting as equals around a table. It wasn't that way at all.

"And when the different people—the Puritans, the bishops—approached the king, they had to do so on their knees. They literally had to crawl up on their hands and knees, and then he would dispense his views to them. So this is really a contradictory thing. We have a king who appears to be listening to other people and wanting to take their views into account, but he is really using the occasion to stamp his own authority."

—Lucy Worsley
Chief Curator; Historic Royal Palaces, London, England

Hampton Court Palace, with formal garden. Courtesy of Steve Porter, photographer.

Thomas Cranmer. Courtesy of The Bridgeman Art Library.

He was a clever man with a talent for debate and dispute, yet nothing was really proposed in any plenipotentiary form, among some forty proposals offered.

Only on the second and last day were the four Puritan delegates brought before their king, somewhat cowed by the munificence of Hampton Court, but ready to join the discussion with many a complaint. They didn't like the vestments they saw the clergy wearing right there in their presence. They didn't like accoutrements and accessories, such as the use of a wedding ring in the marriage ceremony, which they considered idolatrous—a Catholic embellishment. Their complaints continued, in the name of scriptural plain living, until John Rainolds raised his evangelical call for a new translation of the scriptures themselves.

And that, at the last hour of the conference, is the one and only proposal that received King James's immediate, if mediated approval. Yet it was never on any agenda.

James was a very politic man who did not always divulge his most inward motives, and under all the spendor of Hampton Court, he had one preoccupying interest: the divine right of kings, most particularly his own divine right over his expanding Church of England. In this regard, he already had reason to be doubly concerned. First, he had long experienced the sharpness of Calvinistic supervision; at the age of two, as the young King James VI, he watched the Puritans drive his own mother, Mary Queen of Scots, from her throne. Later, the Puritans were instrumental in her execution by a reluctant Queen Elizabeth.

Second, King James himself was about to face the threat of the Gunpowder Plot, an improbable but "proven" Catholic conspiracy to blow

"It is very true. It is ironical that Thomas More and Thomas Cranmer, who enforce royal authority, both end up being the victims of it. They both came to quite a sorry end because of their actions. Thomas More eventually refused to form the Church of England. He fell afoul of Henry VIII in doing that, and Thomas Cranmer, who had been Henry VIII's greatest ally in setting up the Church of England, fell afoul of Mary I. So both of them were martyrs to their beliefs, if you like. Both of them had been the friends and the supporters of kings and queens, but ended up executed by them."

—Lucy Worsley
Chief Curator, Historic Royal Palaces, London, England

up his parliament in 1605 with thirty-six barrels of black powder in the cellarage of the House of Lords. He not only faced religious dissent from the Puritans, but seeming terrorist conspiracy from the Catholics. So long as he retained control over such willfully contrary actions by either renegade Roman papists or reformers who clung too closely to the Geneva Bible, the rest could be better, and more safely, left to committee.

That is exactly what he did after the call for a new English Bible, as reported by William Barlow in *The Summe and Substance of the Conference Which It Pleased His Excellent Majesty to Have With the Lords, Bishops, and Other of His Clergy*. He wanted "one uniforme translation . . . and that this bee done by the best learned in both the Universities, after them to bee reviewed by the Bishops, and the Chiefe learned of the Church . . . and lastly to bee ratified by his Royall authoritie." He then arranged for the fifty-four designated members of his committee to receive forty copies of

Guy Fawkes before King James, 1869–1870 (watercolor on paper), painting by Sir John Gilbert (1817–1897). Harrogate Museums and Arts, North Yorkshire, UK. © Harrogate Museums and Arts, The Bridgeman Art Library.

"King James had been interested in Bible translation for quite a while before he came to England. He had actually suggested it to the Church of Scotland. And I think not just because he wanted a new translation, but from a slightly more political motive: if the energies of his clergy were diverted into translating the Bible, they would stop being so awkward to then King James VI.

"And that was very true in Scotland, and more so when he came to England because he was faced with more Puritans, who might cause trouble in the Church of England, which he found he really liked. So one thing he could give them—without giving them other concessions—was to say, 'Let's translate the Bible, afresh. Let's have a new translation.' And it worked. This really did divert the energy of some people, who might have otherwise been troublesome . . . into a very good cause."

—Diarmaid MacCulloch
Professor DM, University of Oxford, England

The King James translators pored over, read aloud, and examined Hebrew, Greek, German, and Latin Bibles and especially William Tyndale's works to produce the most accurate and authoritative Bible to date.

the latest Bishops' Bible, pages unbound, for their perusal, revision, and improvement, and told them, *Go to!*

For once, during this rare time in academic world history, they formed a really good committee. It was divided into six "companies," impaneled as study groups of nine members each—two companies from Oxford and two from Cambridge, then two from Westminster itself, as Anglican Church headquarters. They divided the total Bible into half a dozen sections. One Oxford panel took on the "four, or greater prophets," Lamentations, and "the twelve lesser prophets," while the other Oxford panel did the Gospels, Acts, and Revelations. At Cambridge, one panel revised "From the First of the Chronicles, with the rest of the Story, and the Hagiographi, viz. Job, Psalms, Proverbs, Canticles, Ecclesiastes," while the other examined "The Prayer for Manasses and the rest of the Aprocrypha." Then at Westminster, one panel took the Pentateuch to the end of 2 Kings, and the other faced up to the controversial New Testament Epistles, those of Paul in particular.

In the end, forty-seven known men actually filled those fifty-four slots. A few were unknown, and a mysterious "Dr Ravens" probably didn't participate, but most held impressive offices as Oxbridge Fellows, a dozen being heads of their colleges. "The choice of revisers seems to have been determined solely by their fitness," A. W. Pollard notes, "and both parties of the Church were represented by some of their best men." Several participants stand out, especially Lancelot Andrewes, listed as "Mr. Dean of Westminster."

Andrewes was the leading reviser among the clergy from Westminster, head of the company translating the Pentateuch, though he also bore stellar academic credentials. He spoke fifteen modern languages, as well as the classical tongues, and had preached to Queen Elizabeth at St. Paul's Cathedral. She had offered him two bishoprics, which he refused, though he accepted Chichester from King James in 1605, Ely in 1609, and later Winchester in 1619. His brother Roger joined the Cambridge Old Testament company. Together they represented high-styled Anglican governance, much admired by T. S. Eliot in his 1928 tribute *For Lancelot Andrewes*.

But on the Puritan side stood Dr. John Rainolds, president of Corpus Christi, whose shout-out to the king at Hampton Court had started the whole revisionism project. Rainolds was a member of the Oxford Old Testament company. Also included were several bishops—three at the start in 1605 and five more to be selected—but their bishoprics weren't really the point. As the departed Thomas Cranmer had learned long ago about the bishops' institutional procrastination, their delay amounted to "such time as we bishops shall set forth a better translation, which I think

Hampton Court Conference, English School. Private Collection, © Look and Learn, The Bridgeman Art Library.

¶ TO THE MOST HIGH AND MIGHTIE Prince, IAMES by the grace of God King of Great Britaine, France and Ireland, Defender of the Faith, &c.

THE TRANSLATORS OE *THE BIBLE*, wish Grace, Mercie, and Peace, through IESVS CHRIST our LORD.

Great and manifold were the blessings(most dread Soueraigne) which Almighty GOD, the Father of all Mercies, beſtowed vpon vs the people of ENGLAND, when firſt he ſent your Maieſties Royall perſon to rule and raigne ouer vs. For whereas it was the expectation of many, who wiſhed not well vnto our SION, that vpon the ſetting of that bright *Occidentall Starre* Queene ELIZABETH of moſt happy memory, ſome thicke and palpable cloudes of darkeneſſe would ſo haue ouerſhadowed this land, that men ſhould haue bene in doubt which way they were to walke, and that it ſhould hardly be knowen, who was to direct the vnſetled State: the appearance of your MAIESTIE, as of the *Sunne* in his ſtrength, inſtantly diſpelled thoſe ſuppoſed and ſurmiſed miſts, and gaue vnto all that were well affected, exceeding cauſe of comfort; eſpecially when we beheld the gouernment eſtabliſhed in your HIGHNESSE, and your hopefull Seed, by an vndoubted Title, and this alſo accompanied with Peace and tranquillitie, at home and abroad.

But amongſt all our Ioyes, there was no one that more filled our hearts, then the bleſſed continuance of the Preaching of GODS ſacred word amongſt vs, which is that ineſtimable treaſure, which excelleth all the riches of the earth, becauſe the fruit thereof extendeth it ſelfe, not onely to the time ſpent in this tranſitory world, but directeth and diſpoſeth men vnto that Eternall happineſſe which is aboue in Heauen.

Then, not to ſuffer this to fall to the ground, but rather to take it vp, and to continue it in that ſtate, wherein the famous predeceſſour of your HIGHNESSE did leaue it; Nay, to goe forward with the confidence and r

A 2

A rare translators' note to the readers. Published in the original version of the KJV Bible. Courtesy of Joe and Jeanne Groberg Collection, on loan to Special Collections, Brigham Young University–Idaho Library. Kimball Ungerman, photographer.

will not be til a day after doomsday." It was far more important that both Regius professors of Hebrew and Greek from both universities were present with their intellectual prowess.

Of further fascination is the often quite worldly experience that several translators brought to their companies. John Layfield had traveled to the New World to fight the Spanish in Puerto Rico and extolled the island beauty of the Caribbean. George Abbot had written a best-selling guide to the world, sketchily, though as the globe was then known. Hadrian à Saravia was half Flemish, half Spanish. Several committee men had traveled throughout Europe, while others were Arab scholars. And two—William Bedwell and Henry Savile, a courtier-scholar known as "a magazine of learning"—were also learned in mathematics. There was an alcoholic Latinist, Richard "Dutch" Thomson, who was noted among his fellows as "a debosh'd drunken English-Dutchman."

Among the churchmen there was even the scholarly John Overall, dean of St. Paul's, who was said to have spent so much of his life speaking Latin that he had almost forgotten how to speak English.

All gathered together in their respective companies for seven laborious years to try their hand at another "inerrant," thus "uniform" English Bible. Such was the professed purpose of this editorial enterprise, to be based once more on the original Greek and Hebrew texts despite the preexisting Vulgate Latin. But no longer were these scholars limited in their access to renderings of what might be taken to be God's Word. They had such an excess of numerous translations, differing so variously, that sufficient unto the day—as the KJV would soon be saying—is the evil thereof. What they had to do was choose among them, to proceed word by word in order to arrive at an eventual text of nearly eight hundred thousand words. Their task was to decide which words to follow where, and when, and how often, and why.

Their method was to assign scholars to examine each and every word and then submit their individual versions to their colleagues in the company, then across companies, and on up the line. In 1689, posthumously, John Selden described the process in his *Table Talk*, a meeting of the final review board of what was likely twelve revisers, back at Stationer's Hall in London:

The translators in King James's time took an excellent way. That part of the Bible was given to him who was the most excellent in such a tongue (as the Apocrypha to Andrew Downs) and then they met together, and one read the translation, the rest holding in their hands some Bible, either of the learned tongues, or French, Spanish.

This brief description offers a pertinent clue as to what the revisers were deeply interested in achieving, which in turn explains why the process took so long. They spent

seven years reading out loud. Whenever in session as a company, they read to each other from the Bible translation upon which they were currently working. They did not merely exchange drafts, or go over notes, or discuss verbiage, as so many a modern committee is incessantly used to doing. They wanted to hear how each and every passage would sound in English. This practice added a deeper dimension to their collective judgments on the ultimate worth of their proposed translations.

Fundamentally, they were aware that reading might be privately done by the inspired individual believer, but they knew that most often, people would be reading aloud to one another, gathered in churches, chapels, and cathedrals; as people in families, around hearths; and in many

Even though it was illegal to own an English language Bible, the commoners anxiously pored over its words in secret.

"The King James Bible was unique among the English Bibles in the scale on which it was set up. Some of the other translations had had groups of people working on them—the Bishops' Bible, for instance, the official, immediate predecessor of the KJV was done by individual bishops taking individual parts. So it was very variable in quality. They had some rules, as the King James translators had rules, but the result was much more uneven. Fewer people were involved, with no effective complete oversight, even though Bishop Matthew Parker did try to give it oversight, and indeed did a lot of very good work himself. But if we think about the King James, it is the first one that is set up on a grand scale, involving lots of people working together. And then a process that will have other people review their work and finally the whole thing being reviewed by delegates from the individual translation committees. This is a grand scheme, quite unlike anything that applied to previous Bibles and not replicated until we get to the Revised Version in the 1880's."

—David Norton
Professor; Victoria University of Wellington, New Zealand

congregations. They knew well enough that many people still had to be read to, given the true state of literacy, in order to comprehend and come to understand God's Word. But they also knew that believers wished to be read to, that reading was a nurturing, socially and emotionally enriching experience. People, even when reading alone, often read aloud to themselves.

That is why the public affection for the KJV has lasted so long. Even though respect for its high timbre commanded too much respect for too long, affection for the KJV continued because the original revisers paid close attention to the beauty and emotion of the words. The original revisers were extremely mindful of the rhetorical effect the Bible needed to have on parishioners, the echoing English that had to illuminate the Old and New Testaments—often in highly emotional and differing ways. Very fortunately, they had a multiple, if diffuse, canon of prior scriptural readings to choose from along with the patience and knowledge to distinguish the best way to extrapolate the theology.

They also knew that in order to accomplish such an immense intellectual task, they had to address these translations on a grand scale. David Norton argues that King James VI's earlier failure at creating a Scottish Bible made him aware of the large commitment required.

The translators observed fifteen rules in the translation of the Bible, set forth by now Archbishop Richard Bancroft, previously the London bishop. Five of them had real import for the scope and nature of the translation:

> Rule 1: The ordinary Bible read in the Church commonly called the Bishops' Bible, to be followed, and as little altered as the Truth of the original will permit.
> Rule 3: The old Ecclesiastical Words are to be kept, viz. The Word Church not to be translated Congregation Etc.
> Rule 6: No Marginal Notes at all to be affixed, but only for the explanation of the Hebrew or Greek Words, which cannot without some circumlocution, so briefly and fitly be express'd in the Text.
> Rule 7: Such Quotations of Places to be marginally set down as shall serve for the reference of one Scripture to another.

These four rules were closely confining, with Rule 3 restricting terminology to the Latin Vulgate in support of the Six Articles, opposing much that the Geneva Bible (which Bancroft abhorred) advocated by way of reform. But Rule 14 unexpectedly opened the floodgates wide.

Clerics used many different Bibles to preach the "Word of God."

Rule 14: These translations to be used when they agree better with the Text than the Bishops: Tindoll's, Matthews, Coverdale's, Whitchurch's, Geneva.

This launched the intense debates, said Ward Allen, that characterized "the steps which the translators followed in preparing their revision."

Each translator completed his revision of a chapter week by week, and each company forged a common revision by comparing these private revisions. The revision being completed, a company circulated its work, book by book, among the other companies. From this circulation, there resulted revisions, made in light of the objection made to the work of a company, and an excursus upon any objection which the original company did not agree to. Then the translators circulated their work among the learned men, who were not official translators, and revised their work in view of the suggestions from these men. Now the translators had to circulate these revisions among the other companies. Then, they prepared a final text. This final text they submitted to the general meeting in London, which spent nine months compounding disagreements among companies.

The KJV translation was approved in 1611 and printing began immediately. Officially printed in 1611–1612, it gradually grew into the standard (through correction of misspellings, printer's errors, and other mishaps) and has endured for four hundred years.

"I think they were enormously able. In fact, they had many advantages, having worked at, particularly, Latin and Greek from childhood, and many of them having learned Hebrew very early in their lives. My sense is that the translators of King James' times were as good, probably better, than most that we have today."

—David Norton
Professor, Victoria University of Wellington, New Zealand

They were slow getting started until 1607. Even Lancelot Andrewes admits to shirking his duties: "But this afternoon is our translation time, and most of our company is negligent, I would have seen you," he wrote an absent friend, then resolved, "but no translation shall hinder me, if once I may understand I commit no error in coming." Once they truly got underway, however, the companies set a fierce pace. Ward Allen remarked on notes taken from disputes over 453 pivotal points

Reading the Bible at St. Paul's English School (nineteenth century). Private Collection, © Look and Learn, The Bridgeman Art Library.

among the Westminster company reviewing the controversial Epistles:

That we know that members of the meeting engaged in arguments, which were sometimes violent, consulted dictionaries, pored over and discussed current and antique theologians, traced textual variations, studied classical authors to settle questions of diction, thought about style, composed in places original readings. We know . . . that the meeting deliberated over questions which were so difficult that the translators themselves had reached a deadlock over correct answers. In light of this, thirty-two discussions . . . provided a full day's work.

Given Rule 14, it should be noted that although the Rheims was not among those alternate versions approved, it must surely have been among those brought into these disputes. Ward Allen observed that "the Rheims New Testament furnished to the Synoptic Gospels and Epistles in the [KJV] as many revised readings as any other version." Where conflict arose that couldn't be solved, there often had to be ambiguous compromise. For instance, at Romans 8:6, Paul's phrase "to be carnally minded" in the Geneva is supported by marginal notes "so explicit that the most careless of readers is put on his guard against dualistic heresies." But Rule 7 allowed no marginal notes except to define Greek or Hebrew terms, so the KJV uses Tyndale's "carnal" phrasing but marginally defines the Greek literally as "the minding of the flesh," an altogether ambiguous dodge. Allen continued:

Individual translators laboured day after day over sheets from the Bishops' Bible. For three years they gathered weekly to compare what they had done. During that three years the Westminster company revised the 121 chapters of the New Testament epistles. They made

"The King James Bible was intended to be read by His priests to their congregations. So every single word of those 700,000 words was read out loud at Stationer's Hall, and the committee listened and checked that it sounded good. And that is part of the reason why it has this amazing orotund language. It is wrong to be reading it. You should be listening to it."

—Lucy Worsley
Chief Curator; Historic Royal Palaces, London, England

4,131 changes, of which 1,344 were readings of their own invention . . . at the rate of twenty-three changes a week, a careful pace when it is born in mind that most of the changes are not radical. But there was other work to do. Each company read the work of all the other companies. Manuscripts were prepared and sent out . . . returned . . . and revised . . . called in. During the year 1609, the Westminster company reviewed the text in light of revisions suggested by the learned men from far and wide. That work completed, the general meeting in London settled the disagreements among companies, this work requiring nine months.

"This was a massive scholarly enterprise. This was no longer a time when one man, like Tyndale, could have done the job. Even if there had been a man around with Tyndale's linguistic gifts and genius, it would have been impossible."

—Guido Latre
Professor; University of Louvain and Ghent, Belgium

At the last, scholars John Nielson and Royal Skousen found in 1998 by computer analysis that Tyndale's contributions to the KJV are some 83 percent of its New Testament and 67 percent of its Old Testament. But behind those percentages is an incomparable "feeling," as Daniell adds, that "the rhythm, vocabulary, and cadence . . . so exquisite and so direct" is rooted in the English language, brought forth out of Tyndale's original sacrifice and genius.

chapter 10

THE WORD OF GOD,
IN THE KING'S ENGLISH

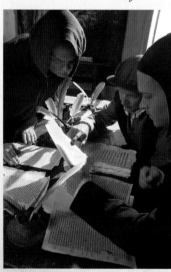

Translators at work on the KJV.

What could King James finally hold in his hands for his royal approval, since he never did "authorize" his Bible? (In fact, even the original manuscript is lost, completely disappeared, very likely into the trash at the several print shops that carelessly handled first publication.)

As it plainly says on its title page, the KJV was only "appointed to be read in Churches," whereas the Bishops' Bible had been both "authorized and appointed to be read in the Churches." Come to think of it, in contrast to the regal Henry and the more demure Elizabeth, James isn't even there on his title page, which is devoted solely to biblical figures. The title page features four Gospel writers, each to a corner: Moses with his tablets and Aaron with his rod, each to a columnar side; then other disciples and apostles elsewhere. They all stand crowded into niches, onto pediments along a forbidding frontal wall, where God reigns at the summit only by His Hebrew initials, the Tetragrammaton (YHWH). How did this Bible somehow eventually come to be the all-assumptive AV—the "Authorized Version" that never was, of course, authorized?

"The Bible," says Diarmaid MacCulloch, scoring a telling point, "is not a book. It is a library of books—a huge cacophony of voices which stretch over thousands of years. And I think that is one of the problems in dealing with this Bible because people think it is a book, and it isn't. It is the result of reflection on God, encounters with God, from so many different peoples, so many different centuries."

So the KJV has served us as a library, assembled by incomparable scholars, severally expert on the Word of God. Its approval came not through any one monarch, but by an inherent assumption of developing rightness over sacrificial time—*Newly Translated out of the Originall tongues & with the former Translations diligently compared and revised by his Majesties Special Comadement*—and by its longevity in print over so many later decades, presently comprising four biblical centuries. This process, starting its crescendo in the late eighteenth century, has come to be nicknamed "Avolatry," a sentimental form of worshipfulness based on an ever-growing myth that has elevated these early seventeenth-century scholars—and their estimable early sources—to heights of spiritual inspiration.

But the KJV did not gain any such immediate prominence, especially over the Geneva Bible.

Begin with the sad acknowledgment that there are always going to be misprints, even in Bibles—and that some of them may be deliberate. It so happens that early editions of the KJV were plagued by them as well as by financial scandal that might have helped precipitate those errors. Robert Barker—the royal printer whom the churchmen struggled so hard to protect commercially—went bankrupt after many lawsuits, some of which included charges of adultery. But the factors that caused the most conflict were egregious printer's errors.

Unhappily, the first two issues of 1611 and 1613 had mixups, dropped lines, spelling errors, and other wild mistakes. There were "She Bibles" and "He Bibles," depending on whether the corrupt text brought "he" or "she" into the city at Ruth 3:15. Since it was Ruth, "She" finally won out. Better yet, the same Bible had "Judas" in for "Jesus" at the Last Supper in Matthew 26:36.

Later there came the "Forgotten Sins" Bible (1638), where at Luke 7:47 "her sins which are many were forgotten" instead of "forgiven." Then came the "Unrighteous" Bible (1653), which asked at 1 Corinthians 6:9, "Know ye not that the unrighteous shall inherit the kingdom of God." But surely the worst was the "Wicked" Bible (1631) that celebrated God's "greatnesse" at Deuteronomy 5:24: "And ye said, Behold, the Lord our God showed us his glory, and his great asse." In the same edition, Exodus 20:14 printed this Seventh Commandment: "Thou shalt commit adultery." For what was adjudged a skulking act, the King's Printers—that is, "Barker and [as]signs of Bill"—were fined an astonishing 300 pounds, and the whole printing

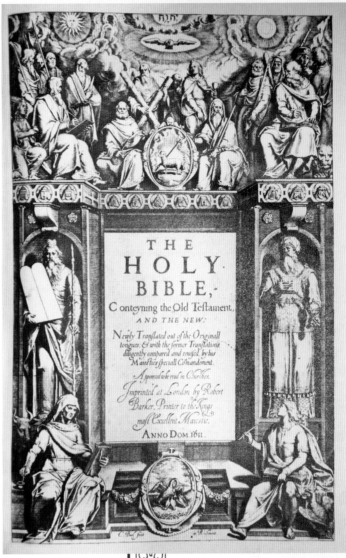

Title pages to these early Bibles were works of art in their detail and imagery, like this title page from the King James Bible. Courtesy of Joe and Jeanne Groberg Collection, on loan to Special Collections, Brigham Young University–Idaho Library. Kimball Ungerman, photographer.

King James I of England and VI of Scotland, by unknown artist. Courtesy Wikimedia Commons.

was recalled. It made for larking off-market resales, but Barker was left utterly ruined.

The devout, churchgoing English public, however, could stand only so much riotous mishap bordering on blasphemy, especially once the Oxbridge presses became involved in this potentially lucrative publishing venture. An intellectual urge arose to correct the inferior print quality, outdated words, minor grammatical errors, and, above all, confused passages of the 1611 KJV itself. Ambrose Ussher—brother of Bishop James Ussher, who fixed those absurd dates for biblical world history—wrote another entire Bible, but who would care to publish it? Then, in 1752, Dr. F. E. Paris of Cambridge worked at revising the KJV until, in 1769, Benjamin Blayney further revised Paris and published in Oxford a standardized Bible known as the Benjamin Blayney Bible. Blayney's Bible suddenly became the "Authorized Version" for the next one hundred years, using James Ussher's infamously limiting A.D. and B.C. dating of world chronology—still used, despite Darwin, in differently driven formulations today.

Likewise in 1769, the great actor David Garrick staged his grand "restoration" of Shakespeare (our first case of "Bardolatry") with his own *Hamlet* (much cut, including most of its bloody last act). That summer, there was an over-costumed festival in a sleepy, rural backwater called Stratford-on-Avon. The festivities lasted three days, full of cultural celebration, including Avolatry, and James Boswell attended as an armed Corsican chief *bandito*. The last day it poured and flooded out even the swans. But it was proclaimed here that the KJV—and those who translated

Printing History

"The man responsible for printing the Bible was a monopolist—the King's Printer, previously, the Queen's Printer—Robert Barker, and he underwent all the expenses of printing the Bible, but didn't in fact recoup his money. He was a bad businessman. Nevertheless the office of the King's Printer remained the one office that could officially print the Bible. This expanded in 1629, when Cambridge University Press exercised a right given to them by Henry VIII to print anything, effectively. So they came in and printed a Cambridge Paragraph Bible that became the second official guardian of the text of the King James Version. And then later on, Oxford University acquired the right to print Bibles and became the third official guardian of the KJV. Oxford was the last of these three to come in and eventually did the most important edition of the Bible that settled the text we now have. That edition came out in 1769, essentially finishing off textual development work carried on principally in Cambridge. So the text we now read is that 1769 text prepared by Benjamin Blayney."

—David Norton

"Gutenberg is printing in the middle of the 15th century. His first production amounted to less than 200 books. Within two generations Martin Luther could publish a pamphlet, in print, that in a year would sell 250,000 copies. Printed books were revolutionary in the 16th century." Courtesy of FIRES OF FAITH; Plantin-Moretus Museum, Groberg Films and BYU Broadcasting, Steve Porter, photographer.

its sacred texts—were especially "venerated" from that moment forward for the work they completed back in 1611.

What King James initially might have held in his hands, printed for him by Robert Barker, was an evolving Authorized Version. It had taken another century and a half for its status as the AV to even begin.

That original KJV was already somewhat distant in outlook. It had to be, given the nature of its compendious task of inclusion and the clarion call for royal order from the past Elizabethan establishment, now turned Jacobean. The companies fully understood. Among other roles it would play, the King James Bible stood as the anointed rival of the Geneva Bible.

As champion of such a righteous cause, its numbered verses pass melodiously with an establishmentarian tempo, and many of its passages are hauntingly beautiful. They are made beautiful through the passionate contributions of its previous translators, restored to this Bible by the collective will of knowledgeable scholars. But its conservative grammar, weighted toward Latin and Anglican practices, was kept largely in place, so that this KJV could authoritatively embrace eighty different biblical books. It had to be a Bible that contained, as Daniell points out, "a rich variety of styles, within one set of covers, from the Hebrew and Greek of its originals." Its Hebrew Old Testament ranges from epic glory and victory ballads to congregational prayer—from religious meditation, proverbial wisdom, and erotic lyricism to intense prophecy, in multiple prophetic voices. Genesis alone moves from the mundane to the surreal, all within the Garden of Eden and beyond. The later Greek New Testament, on the other hand, covers the mission of Christ's gospel journey on earth through the philosophical turnings of Paul's subtle mind to the apocalyptic chaos of Revelations. And all this had to be done solely—given Rule 15— in common English.

This meant inevitably that they had to allow some distancing, a flattening out of presentation to suit all these extreme demands. "KJV was born archaic: it was intended as a step back," writes Daniell. That is what was done to make it sound biblical. That is why the Bishops' Bible, even though thrice-removed from its sources, was chosen as "the good book" to be made "better," in order that its antique formulaics and repetitions and the "in the beginnings," "it came to passes," "begats,"

Portrait of James Boswell (1740–1795) by Sir Joshua Reynolds (1723–1792). In 1769, Boswell celebrated the KJV as the "Authorized Version" at actor David Garrick's first-ever Shakespearian festival at Stratford-on-Avon. Courtesy Wikimedia Commons.

English Hexapla (six versions on two pages). Courtesy of Joe and Jeanne Groberg Collection, on loan to Special Collections, Brigham Young University–Idaho Library. Kimball Ungerman, photographer.

"beholds," and "amens" could somehow keep everything so mystically wired somehow ecclesiastically together.

There are three explanations for this theological stepping-back. First, it reset the standard for the middle-of-the-road Anglican establishment, historically sought since Henry VIII handed down the rites and regulations on divine revelation (*Verbum Dei*, or "Word of God") in 1533–1534. Second, its inherent Latin structurally carried a fifteen-hundred-year assurance of abiding Christian faith, with all the authority of settled belief. (Remember, there are still those today in Christendom who prefer the "original text," meaning the Vulgate, though even the Catholic Mass has recently undergone revisions in English.) Third, and fundamentally, the Christian world—*sub species aeternitatis*, "under the aspect of eternity"—is divided between those who think that holy scripture should always be elevated above the common buzz—with an air of sanctity, however remote from real life—and those who believe that since the whole point of the Incarnation was that God became human, often among the local lowlife, and just as the Greek is common, ordinary English is to be freely spoken here. The first prefer "Judge not," the second "Jesus said . . ." In the seventeenth century, Anglican politics preferred to "keep a worshipful distance." Thus KJV's Jacob "lay with" Leah in Genesis 30:16, while Tyndale has him "sleep with" her.

Not that the KJV's revisers didn't sometimes wield a deft pen of their own. Even following Tyndale and Geneva, they added memorable words. Tyndale has Jesus saying, "Suffer the children to come unto me," but in Mark 10:14, the revisers immortally made that, "Suffer the little children. . . ." In Matthew 22:14, they changed Tyndale's "Many are called and few be chosen"—with assists from Coverdale and Geneva—to "Many are called, but few are chosen." In Romans 8:31, they straightened out Tyndale's "If God be on our side: who can be against us?" to read "If God be for us. . . ?" paying, for once, a compliment to the Catholic source. And always remember that the revisers, despite other Pauline doctrine, chose *caritas* from the Latin and carried "faith, hope, and charity" from the Bishops' Bible hard into the KJV.

And within that triplet came another KJV triumph. Most recently, Robert Pogue Harrison, a Stanford professor, wisely discriminated among several biblical definitions of Pauline "faith" from the first chapter of Hebrews. What basically defines faith depends primarily on the translation of the Greek word *hypostasis*, meaning "standing under" (*hypo*, under + *stasis*, stand = *histasthai*, the middle voice of *histanai*, cause to stand—hence, that which is under + stood).

Tyndale originally wrote: "Faith is the sure confidence of things, which are hoped for, & a certainty of things which are not seen."

The Geneva declared: "Now faith is the ground of things, which are hoped for, and the evidence of things that are not seen."

But the King James Version states: "Now faith is the substance of things hoped for, the evidence of things not seen."

Not only did the KJV translators edit out the unnecessary verbiage ("which are"), but their choice of the key word, as Harrison writes, was "brilliant." *Sub* + *stance* is the equivalent in its Latin roots of the English "under" + "stood." And the word itself carries other substantial echoes of religious doctrine, including the debate over "transubstantiation" of the wafer blessed by the priest during Mass.

There are other such defining, subtle touches, and among a total of 258 famous English phrasings that occur in the KJV, eighteen of them are original to these revisers. *National Geographic* recently ran a search to find the twenty-five most oft-continuing usages. The most prominently recognized phrase is "From time to time" (Ezek. 4:10), followed by "The root of the matter" (Job 19:21), "Stand in awe" (Ps. 4:4), "Get thee behind me" (Luke 4:8), "Suffer the little children" (Luke 18:16), "As a lamb to the slaughter" (Isa. 53:7), "A thorn in the flesh" (2 Cor. 12:7), and "How the mighty are fallen" (2 Sam. 1:19). Those are followed, in no particular order, by "A still small voice" (1 Kgs. 19:12), "Turned the world upside down" (Acts 17:6), "Unto the pure all things are pure" (Titus 1:15), "Know for a certainty" (Josh. 23:13), "A man after his own heart" (1 Sam. 13:14), "No

Latin Vulgate Bible. Courtesy of Joe and Jeanne Groberg Collection, on loan to Special Collections, Brigham Young University–Idaho Library. Kimball Ungerman, photographer.

though not in vertue, yet in power: and by his power and wisdome he built a Temple to the LORD, such a one as was the glory of the land of Israel, and the wonder of the whole world. But was that his magnificence liked of by all? We doubt of it. Otherwise, why doe they lay it in his sonnes dish, and call vnto him for || easing of the burden, *Make*, say they, *the grieuous seruitude of thy father, and his sore yoke, lighter.* Belike he had charged them with some leuies, and troubled them with some cariages; Hereupon they raise vp a tragedie, and wish in their heart the Temple had neuer bene built. So hard a thing it is to please all, euen when we please God best, and doe seeke to approue our selues to euery ones conscience.

The highest personages haue bene calumniated.

If we will descend to later times, wee shall finde many the like examples of such kind, or rather vnkind acceptance. The first Romane Emperour did neuer doe a more pleasing deed to the learned, nor more profitable to posteritie, for conseruing the record of times in true supputation; then when he corrected the Calender, and ordered the yeere according to the course of the Sunne: and yet this was imputed to him for noueltie, and arrogancie, and procured to him great obloquie. So the first Christened Emperour (at the leastwise that openly professed the faith himselfe, and allowed others to doe the like) for strengthening the Empire at his great charges, and prouiding for the Church, as he did, got for his labour the name *Pupillus,* as who would say, a wastefull Prince, that had neede of a Guardian, or ouerseer. So the best Christened Emperour, for the loue that he bare vnto peace, thereby to enrich both himselfe and his subiects, and because he did not seeke warre but find it, was iudged to be no man at armes, (though indeed he excelled in feates of chiualrie, and shewed so much when he was prouoked) and condemned for giuing himselfe to his ease, and to his pleasure. To be short, the most learned Emperour of former times, (at the least, the greatest politician) what thankes had he for cutting off the superfluities of the lawes, and digesting them into some order and method? This, that he hath bene blotted by some to be an Epitomist, that is, one that extinguished worthy whole volumes, to bring his abridgements into request. This is the measure that hath bene rendred to excellent Princes in former times, euen, *Cum bene facerent, male audire,* For their good deedes to be euill spoken of. Neither is there any likelihood, that enuie and malignitie died, and were buried with the ancient. No, no, the reproofe of *Moses* taketh hold of most ages; *You are risen vp in your fathers stead, an increase of sinfull men. What is that that hath bene done? that which shall be done: and there is no new thing vnder the Sunne,* saith the Wiseman: and S. *Steuen, As your fathers did, so doe you.* This, and more to this purpose, His Maiestie that now reigneth (and long, and long may he reigne, and his offspring for euer, *Himselfe and children and childrens children alwayes*) knew full well, according to the singular wisedome giuen vnto him by God, and the rare learning and experience that he hath attained vnto; namely that whosoeuer attempteth any thing for the publike (specially if it appertaine to Religion, and to the opening and clearing of the word of God) the same setteth himselfe vpon a stage to be glouted vpon by euery euil eye, yea, he casteth himselfe headlong vpon pikes, to be gored by euery sharpe tongue. For he that medleth with mens Religion in any part, medleth with their custome, nay, with their freehold, and though they find no content in that which they haue, yet they cannot abide to heare of altering. Notwithstanding his Royall heart was not daunted or discouraged for this or that cooler, but stood resolute, *as a statue immoueable, and an anuile not easie to be beaten into plates,* as one sayth; he knew who had chosen him to be a Souldier, or rather a Captaine, and being assured that the course which he intended made much for the glory of God, and the building vp of his Church, he would not suffer it to be broken off for whatsoeuer speeches or practises. It doth certainely belong vnto Kings, yea, it doth specially belong vnto them, to haue care of Religion, yea, to know it aright, yea, to professe it zealously, yea, to promote it to the vttermost of their power. This is their glory before all nations which meane well, and this will bring vnto them a farre most excellent weight of glory in the day of the Lord Iesus. For the Scripture saith not in vaine, *Them that honour me, I will honour,* neither was it a vaine word that *Eusebius* deliuered long agoe, that pietie towards God was the weapon, and the onely weapon that both preserued *Constantines* person, and auenged him of his enemies.

His Maiesties constancie, notwithstanding calumniation, for the suruey of the English translations.

But now what pietie without trueth? what trueth (what sauing trueth) without the word of God? what word of God (whereof we may be sure) without the Scripture? The Scriptures we are commanded to search. Ioh.5.39. Esa.8.20. They are commended that searched & studied them. Act.17.11. and 8.28,29. They are reproued that were vnskilful in them, or slow to beleeue them. Mat.22.29. Luk.24.25. They can make vs wise vnto saluation. 2.Tim.3.15. If we be ignorant, they will instruct vs; if out of the way, they will bring vs home; if out of order, they will reforme vs; if in heauines, comfort vs; if dull, quicken vs; if colde, inflame vs. *Tolle, lege, Tolle, lege,* Take vp and read, take vp and read the Scriptures, (for vnto them was the direction) it was said vnto S. *Augustine* by a supernaturall voyce. *Whatsoeuer is in the Scriptures, beleeue me,* saith the same S. *Augustine, is high and diuine, there is verily trueth, and a doctrine most fit for the refreshing and renewing of mens minds, and truely so tempered, that euery*

The praise of the holy Scriptures.

Marginal references: enochymian, 1.King.12.4. — C.Cæsar. Plutarch. — Constantine. — Aurel.Victor. Theodosius. Zosimus. — Iustinian. — Numb.32.14. Eccles.1.9. Act.7.51. — Suidas. — 1.Sam.2.30. — Eusebius lib.10 cap.8. — S.August.confess lib.8,ca.12. S.August.de vtilit.credendi cap.6.

The statement of the translators to the reader, without the slate sheet. Courtesy of Joe and Jeanne Groberg Collection, on loan to Special Collections, Brigham Young University–Idaho Library. Kimball Ungerman, photographer.

small stir" (Acts 12:18), "Lay up for yourselves treasures in heaven" (Matt. 6:20), "East of Eden" (Gen. 4:16), "Much study is a weariness of the flesh" (Eccl.12:12), "Set thine house in order" (Isa. 38:1), "Fell flat on his face" (Num. 22:31), "Beat their swords into ploughshares" (Isa. 2:4), "Pour out your heart" (Ps. 62:8), "To everything there is a season" (Eccl. 3:1), "The skin of our teeth" (Job 19:20), "Be horribly afraid" (Jer. 2:12), "Let us now praise famous men" (the Apocrypha's Ecclesiasticus 44:1), and "Put words in his mouth" (Ex. 4:15), which is just what we've been doing here.

But sometimes, one finds that meddling only mars. In Matthew 26:41, Tyndale's "The spirit is willing but the flesh is weak" was raised— by adding one supererogatory word: "indeed"—to a pompous slogan. That again comes from Rheims via the Vulgate, and the binding word forces distance and formality upon what Jesus said to calm His own fearful disciples during that terrifying night in Gethsemane. It is church Latin in all its pomposity, a "judge not" moment. In contrast, Tyndale was speaking common English throughout his colloquial biblical lore that was expanded through the Geneva Bible to come down to us through the King James Version.

We hear such a multitude of memories from the KJV; every Bible story carries their awing echo. "They heard the voice of the Lord God walking in the garden in the cool of the day" (Gen. 3). "God shall wipe away all tears from their eyes" (Rev. 7:17). "My days are swifter than a weaver's shuttle" (Job 7:6). "How art thou fallen from heaven, O Lucifer, son of the morning!" (Isaiah 14:2). "In him we live, and move, and have our being" (Acts 17:28). "Behold, I stand at the door, and knock" (Rev. 3:20).

Other phrases anciently composed now bear the proverbial mark of Cain: modern anomie that violate social or moral standards. "Am I my brother's keeper?" (Gen. 4); "I am escaped with the skin of my teeth" (Job 19:20); "saying Peace, peace; when there is no peace" (Jer. 8:11); "For they have sown the wind, and they shall reap the whirlwind" (Hosea 8:7); "the signs of the times" (Matt. 16:3); "fell among thieves" (Luke 10:30); "a law unto themselves" (Rom. 2:14); "wages of sin" (Rom. 6:23); "all things to all men" (1 Cor. 9:22); and "filthy lucre"(1 Tim. 3:3). But then we happily come upon "perfect love casteth out fear" (1 John 4:18).

Occasionally an estranging loss of character occurs with too much tightening of the narrative, so that even the Bible risks losing its real story line. In Genesis 3, Eve is listening to the serpent discuss the forbidden fruit hanging low from the tree of knowledge of good and evil. She is fearful that, as God has forewarned, partaking of the fruit will cause her death. In the KJV, the serpent prissily tells Eve that in his considered opinion, "Ye shall not surely die" (Gen. 3:4). But Tyndale sounds as if he must have overheard from the bushes what the serpent really said. "Tush," he hisses to deceive her, "ye shall not die."

Nevertheless, the KJV gradually succeeded, even over its earliest flawed printings, in gaining a readership through its majestic embrace of Tyndale and its capture of Coverdale's grace notes, with much help from John Rogers and many another reforming pen who, like Luther, fought the devil with ink and sometimes died for what they believed they had inked: the Word of God. The KJV eventually replaced even the popular Geneva Bible among English-speaking people, but only after the King James Bible had inherited much of what the Geneva held sacred, minus its notes.

Closeup of woodblock print of "Paradise Before the Fall." Courtesy of Harold B. Lee Special Collections, BYU Library. Kimball Ungerman, photographer.

"King James' actual history is complicated. Later views on King James, however, were anything but complicated. In 1911, one of the longest reviews of the King James Bible said of the King: 'He was perverse, pedantic and tyrannical. Moreover, the immorality of his court was matched only by the imbecility of his politics.' And this same author went on to say, 'No one was more responsible for the production of this classic of English literature, than King James.'"

—Mark Noll
Professor of History; University of Notre Dame, Indiana

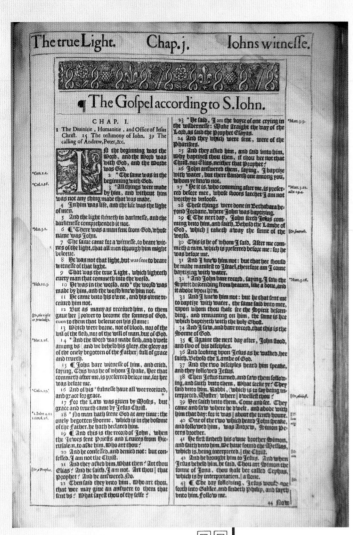

A page from the 1613 King James "She" Bible. Courtesy of Joe and Jeanne Groberg Collection, on loan to Special Collections, Brigham Young University–Idaho Library. Kimball Ungerman, photographer.

Diarmaid MacCulloch believes the precise window of time when the KJV was translated through 1611 was "a sort of stroke of luck." He writes, "The Church of England was doing pretty well, when even Puritans would grudgingly say, 'Well, it's not such a bad Church after all.' You have got a Protestant monarch in Scotland and England, and all those things worked together to make this very much King James's Bible. Now his son, King Charles I, was much less popular; in fact, he caused the English Civil War. But somehow the KJV never became King Charles' Bible. By the time King Charles had been executed, and Oliver Cromwell was briefly ruling England as Puritan head of the Commonwealth, Cromwell actually authorized printings of the KJV. So this Bible was becoming the Bible of all English speakers and all Scottish/English speakers too. All this occurred in a very narrow window of luck, and that is initially why the KJV stuck."

Yet its eventual triumph came out of a perverse inspiration that struck a monarch while sitting in state on his very throne.

chapter 11

THE KING JAMES BIBLE

'ROUND THE GIRDLED EARTH

Once Avolatry began to flourish, the KJV grew into a publishing phenomenon that borders on a circulation miracle, akin to the miracle of the loaves and fishes. It became the Authorized Version on little more than its own inner authority plus the uncertain corrections of Benjamin Blayney—the designated AV for more than the next hundred years. As Queen Victoria came into her dominant reign, Her Majesty began distributing copies throughout her empire, delivering Bibles personally to any subject head-of-state to whom she gave audience.

During the nineteenth century, the KJV enjoyed huge worldwide circulation through the missionary activities of the British and Foreign Bible Society (BFBS) as well as through the frontier distribution undertaken by the American Bible Society (ABS). The printing process of stereotyping with papier-mâché mats produced a flood of cheap, readable Bibles—the KJV without the Apocrypha—that reached nearly a million copies adrift eleven years after the BFBS founding in 1804. Two decades later, the volume was so great that the cataloguers Darlow, Moule, and Herbert have since found it impossible to keep count. How many millions beyond millions of reprinted Bibles have circulated globally can only be fantasized, due to laxity and reticence

Coronation portrait of Queen Victoria, 1838, by George Hayter (1792–1871). Courtesy Wikimedia Commons.

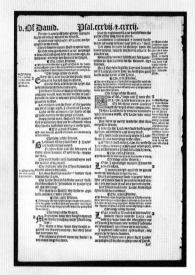

Original page of Tyndale Bible. Courtesy of The Church of Jesus Christ of Latter-day Saints. Kimball Ungerman, photographer.

1613 King James Bible. Courtesy of Harold B. Lee Special Collections, BYU Library. Kimball Ungerman, photographer.

among publishers to reveal their sacred sales figures, so it is far beyond any public accounting ever vainly attempted.

Occasionally, a generalizing graph appears that provides some picture of the magnitude of Bible publication through charting the trends in cities, the number of publishers, and the number of editions of the Bible in the United States, 1777 to 1880. "What we can estimate," Daniell writes, "is the number of new translations into English, since 1526 from the original languages." Through historical retrospect, we gather that some 1,500 Bibles, New Testaments, and single books of Psalms were translated from the Greek and Hebrew through 1900. From better recordkeeping, we can add another 1,500 new translations during the twentieth century. From the first printing of Tyndale's Bible at Worms to the millennial year of 2000, then, there have been 3,000 different translations of God's Word into English from the ancient tongues. But as for any actual sales figures, even on the KJV, those have been kept as secret as any giant oil company's internal accountancy.

More scrupulous regard has been leveled upon the text. As the AV, the KJV was kept under close watch—the last thorough Victorian vetting of some 1,500 misprints was the Cambridge Paragraph Bible completed by F. H. Scrivener in 1873—to assure that the Bible always returned to the lectern whole and all the more welcome. The Cambridge Bible was never officially challenged until 1885, once the Anglican Church had completed its Revised Version, followed by a similar American Standard Version promulgated in 1901.

Work on the RV was launched in 1870 by Dr. Samuel Wilberforce, bishop of Winchester, who was not regarded as competent to undertake the task. T. H. Huxley, the defender of evolution, said he'd rather be descended from a humble monkey than Bishop Wilberforce, and the bishop did not enjoy the support of many of his Anglican clergy. The course of that agonized English revision—through fifteen years of two "companies" in Westminster once again attempting to correct both the Old and the New Testaments with large worry over the Epistles—was never happy.

This is not the place to review the carnage, but the battle was essentially over new scholarship from Cambridge (especially the work of B. F. Westcott and F. J. A. Holt) that had advanced critical knowledge of the underlying Greek text previously ignored against a stubborn defense of the KJV, led stalwartly by Dr. Scrivener. David Norton argues that "the RV [Revised Version] was a compromise between the irresistible need to revise and the immovable monument" of the King James Bible. This caused an overwhelming reaction among far-flung believers against the RV. They did not like so many petty changes—more than 36,000—to update the language, nor such threatening shifts as moving material from Luke to the margins. Note the following ironic edit: "Some ancient authorities omit: 'And Jesus said, Father, forgive them; for they know not what they do.'" Their greatest dislike was the change in the Lord's Prayer from "deliver us from evil" to "deliver us from the evil one." There was also much questioning of why our Savior's name had been switched from Christ to the Messiah. Why then call His followers "Christians" in the first place?

Still, initial sales were a runaway on both sides of the Atlantic. The advance was one million copies. Two Chicago newspapers had the text telegraphed and published the entire RV that Sunday. In New York, almost four hundred Bibles sold in the first few days, and in less than a year, three million were purchased in the United Kingdom and the United States.

The subsequent outcry was long and loud, but Biblical scholars still insist the RV broke the lock that the *Textus Receptus*—accepted Greek texts of the New Testament—had on sound translation, thus opening the way to greater accuracy, even over Tyndale's literary genius. A Revised Standard Version (RVS) was done in 1952—this time by an American board of editorial oversight—to more favorable response, and a New Revised Standard Version (NRV) has been available since 1990. Dwight MacDonald, the arch critic of popular "kitsch," had roundly attacked the RSV, back

Geneva Bible page. Courtesy of Joe and Jeanne Groberg Collection, on loan to Special Collections, Brigham Young University–Idaho Library. Kimball Ungerman, photographer.

"It is a common place today to call the King James Bible a literary classic. But as a historian, I am intrigued that almost no one talked much publicly about the shape of the language, the style of the KJB until into the 19th century. So the King James Bible is around for nearly 200 years before Lord McCauley calls it 'A book which, if everything else in our language should perish, would alone suffice to show the extent of its beauty and power.'

"Thomas Carlyle, Samuel Taylor Coleridge, even Charles Dickens began to praise the King James Bible as a literary masterpiece. Myself, I do think it is a literary classic. The Psalms, the Gospels are forceful. They are punchy. The technical word is they used a paratactic style in the prose. But why it took so long to call it a linguistic classic is a question worth pondering.

"My sense is that so long as the Bible was tied up with intense political allegiances, it was easier to focus on the Bible for its religious content than its literary form. In the 17th century, there were these conflicts within the Church of England between the Puritans and the Anglicans—dissenting Puritans off to one side, high church Anglicans way off to another side. For much of the 18th century, the English speaking world is engaged in a deadly conflict with the French monarchy, which, of course, to the English mind represents tyranny. Whereas in their own minds, the English, including the American colonies, are the people of freedom, liberty, and the Bible. In those polemical terms, the Bible was important as a religious document for grounding Protestantism. Only after the end of the great century of warfare with France—Catholic France versus Protestant Britain—is it possible for Victorian England and Victorian America to begin to emphasize the aesthetic character of the translation."

—Mark Noll
Professor of History; University of Notre Dame, Indiana

in the 1950s, but his grounds, however impassioned, were basically literary, even antiquarian. Thomas Nelson Publishers reissued the original 1611 edition packaged as a matching gift with their own modernization of the KJV in 1982, just to show the close affinities and shared graces between two holy scriptures so separated by time. Today, the KJV continues to comprise 15 percent of the American Bible market, and its share in the international market, throughout English-speaking countries and other countries via many translations, is globally significant.

In retrospect, the height of the KJV's eminence came during its popular acceptance throughout English-speaking Protestant churches, regardless of denomination, both in Great Britain and the United States during the nineteenth century. Though it was still chosen primarily as the Word of God, the KJV first began to be acknowledged and extolled in the nineteenth century, particularly among Victorian writers, as "literature."

For a change, let us look to American culture as hinging greatly on the distribution of the KJV, from our very earliest colonial days. If the Pilgrims were temperamentally inclined toward the Geneva Bible, the majority of Massachusetts Bay Puritans—themselves British subjects, basically loyal to king and country—were more organizationally accepting of the KJB. They applied the Bible to all political and social issues, and historian Harry Stout notes that "questions of national polity and social order increasingly received the attention of the learned divines."

That, in fact, is what brought about Cotton Mather's unfortunate involvement in the Salem witch trials. More beneficently, as early as 1663, John Eliot had translated the KJV into an Algonquin Indian Bible for

phonetic use in seeking to convert the first Native Americans to Christianity.

But only after the Revolution and the Constitutional refounding of the United States did the KJV really soar in distribution, largely through the Second Great Awakening of religious fervor in the later nineteenth century. The First Great Awakening had occurred over the late 1730s and early 1740s under the fiery preaching of Jonathan Edwards and others who encouraged unrest throughout New England. Wildly emotional, the revivalism was still an improvement, claimed Ralph Waldo Emerson, over "the corpse-cold Unitarianism of Brattle Street and Harvard College."

Young James Madison chose to stay another year at Princeton University under John Witherspoon, who later signed the Declaration of Independence, to study theology, and those studies affected Madison's own writing of the Constitution. Much legal thinking, including Chief Justice John Marshall's decisions, arguably came from the Bible's

The Puritans carried both the Geneva Bible and the King James Bible to the Massachussetts Bay Colony in America. The Geneva Bible was soon replaced by the official Bible, the King James Bible. Courtesy of Groberg Films, Mark Mabry, photographer.

The British colonists and later the US citizens were eager to hear the word of God preached from the Bible. Courtesy of The Bridgeman Art Library.

Senator Thomas Hart Benton by Matthew Harris Jouett (circa 1820). Courtesy Wikimedia Commons.

perceived underpinning of the common law. Ben Franklin, as usual, was more skeptical of the KJV, and tried rewriting passages to be more easily understood, then gave up when he couldn't convince other readers. But the Second Great Awakening reached out far more broadly through camp meetings organized by the Methodists and Baptists, largely in Kentucky, beginning at Cane Ridge in 1801. Tens of thousands had "an outpouring of the spirit" and launched fervid evangelical commitments, such as the Temperance Movement.

Out of that spiritual awakening, the American Bible Society was started from thirty-four such local societies out of New York in 1816. Until then, Parson Weems—the sermonizing biographer of George Washington's display of honesty over a mythically felled cherry tree—had been your typical, circuit-riding Bible salesman. But by 1800, printing the most up-to-date Bible—the KJV—had turned into a growth industry backed by libraries, reading groups, and the country's schoolmasters and teachers. The ABS promoted sixty different redactions of the KJV in what were then gigantic numbers—three hundred and sixty thousand in 1829, a million annually by the 1860s. Not only was the King James Bible the one basic book throughout all the country's schoolhouses, it was the sole volume that young Abraham Lincoln had for learning to read by frontier firelight.

"Lincoln never joined a church," Mark Noll notes, "almost certainly in his early years he was some kind of skeptic about traditional religion. He came closer to more traditional beliefs, but never professed faith in Christ, as the evangelicals of the period wanted him to do. Yet throughout his political career, he quoted masterfully from the scriptures to make the points he wanted to make."

"A house divided cannot stand," Lincoln declared in 1858, preparing to debate Senator Stephen Douglas across Illinois. That was "rhetorical," Noll admits, but over the course of the Civil War, Lincoln "became more serious" until "the great moment" of his second inaugural address. During this tragic time, from 1850 through 1870, the spread of the King James Bible peaked across the bloody tatters of the torn Union.

"Both sides read the same Bible and pray to the same God," Lincoln said in 1865, "and each invokes His aid against the other." And then he drew upon holy scripture from the King James Bible three times to drive home his tragic but unsparing lesson to the wartime nation: "It may seem strange that any men should dare to ask a just God's assistance in wringing their bread from other men's faces, but let us judge not, that we be not judged." Lincoln's words on judgment came right out of Matthew 7:1, in deft deference to his damnation of slavery as unjustifiable.

Abraham Lincoln, the sixteenth president of the United States. Courtesy Wikimedia Commons.

"The prayers of both could not be answered," Lincoln went on. "That of neither has been answered fully. The Almighty has his own purposes. 'Woe unto the world because of offenses; for it must needs be that offenses come, but woe to that man by whom the offenses cometh.'" Again Lincoln quotes Jesus directly from Matthew 18:7 and similarly from Luke 17:1, for such are the woeful offenses that come by the agency of the slaveholder.

Then Lincoln addressed the unknowable course of God's actions toward His own purposes, despite all that mortals may hope to understand them. "If we shall suppose that American slavery is one of those offenses which, in the providence of God, must needs come, but which, having continued through His appointed time, He now wills to remove, and that He gives to both North and South this terrible war as the woe due to those by whom the offense came, shall we discern

The KJV Bible was a standard text for all Christian faiths in the formative years of the United States. Courtesy of The Bridgeman Art Library.

therein any departure from these divine attributes which the believers in a living God ascribe to Him?"

The answer to that hard question, in Lincoln's troubled view, may remain a mystery, but it will not come down to any cowardly negation. You do not desert God for disappointing your fevered expectations of His proper conduct. As Lincoln's staff found after his murder in jottings on *Meditations on the Divine Will*: "The will of God prevails—In great contests each party claims to act in accordance with the will of God. Both may be, and one must be wrong. God cannot be for, and against the same thing at the same time. In the present civil war it is quite possible that God's purpose is somewhat different from the purpose of either party—yet human instrumentalities, working just as they do, are the best adaption to effect this."

So Lincoln concluded his severe judgment: "Fondly do we hope, fervently do we pray, that this scourge of war will pass away. Yet, if God wills that it continue until all the wealth piled by the bondman's two hundred and fifty years of unrequited toil shall be sunk, and until every drop of blood drawn by the lash shall be paid by another drawn by the sword, as was said three thousand years ago, so still must be said 'the judgments of the Lord are true and righteous altogether.'" It was his third reference, across three biblical millennia, and came straight out of Psalm 19:9. Then his peroration ("With malice toward none, with charity for all") completes this grand homily offered out of what is often called our civic religion, with every chosen word addressing God's purpose out of the KJV.

If that is a sublime moment in our biblically inspired civic religion, it represents a continuing piety throughout the days of our democratic republic, variously observed by every president. George Washington, as father of our country, was strict in his church attendance, but never once took communion. Decades later, Dwight D. Eisenhower, lately pledging allegiance "under God," said that without a belief in God, "the United States of America makes no sense"—then added, "And I don't care which One." Jack Kennedy had to speak conclusively to his strong belief in the "wall of separation" between religion and governmental power. Symbolically, to come full circle, Barack Obama chose to be sworn into office with his hand on Abraham Lincoln's King James Bible.

Yet even Lincoln worried about what he had said in his second inaugural address. As Thurlow Weed congratulated him on his speech, Lincoln replied that his words would not be "immediately popular. Men are not flattered by being shown that there is a difference of purpose between the Almighty and them."

Still, even as an oft-uncertain society, we continually search after some better understanding of God's Word. Simply as a matter of scholarly research, the KJV has been superseded by deeper investigation into newly discovered historical sources, such as the Dead Sea Scrolls. Also, we have developed greater knowledge of past Middle Eastern culture, such that so-called "Jesus studies" have attempted to profile how a living Christ might have realistically ministered among His very human and contemporary followers—and even how a Messiah might be perceived to have risen from His own sepulchre—or not, as many a modern mind chooses to deny.

Of late there has also been complaint against the KJV text on grounds of difficulties with the language and incomprehension among today's readers, not unlike Ben Franklin's own qualms about the KJV. This touches on the difficult choice that faces translators of the Bible: should they pursue a formal translation, in which an equivalent word in English is found for every textual word or phrase in the Hebrew, Greek, or Latin writings? That was the preference in the nineteenth-century corrections through 1885, a practice that has affected later, more scholarly revisionism ever since. But also during the twentieth century, a more general linguistic approach became popular as an equivalent translation, in which the substantial sense of any given passage from the original text is to be rendered by a similar but broader wording in English. We now have a popular Good News Bible (GNB) that takes this wider, more everyday approach, but too often these unrestrained ventures into interpretation risk a spiritual emptiness, with everything biblical left to lie abandoned by the Samarian wayside.

One of the boasts about the GNB is that it shifts "from traditional theological language to language as common as that used in the newspaper." But is it really any improvement, even in clarity, to replace "When the morning

stars (sang) together, and all the sons of God shouted for joy" (Job 38:7) with "In the dawn of that day the stars sang together, and the heavenly beings shouted for joy"? When the shepherds heard the angels from on high that Christmas Eve, were they just "terribly frightened" or more in truth, "sore afraid"? Psalm 91 begins, "He that dwelleth in the secret place of the most High shall abide under the shadow of the Almighty. I will say to the Lord. . . ." Can this be the same revered venue that the GNB describes, "Whoever goes to the Lord for safety, whoever remains under the protection of the Almighty, can say to him. . ."? Is this where I pick up my loan application?

We can take some comfort from the fact that the words of the KJV are still around in the original as well as a very much a continuing presence in the revised texts.

Besides, a literary tradition has existed since Puritan days in American

"The KJV is clearly not lost today. Statistics on Bible sales are notoriously inexact, but the best I've seen suggest that even in the last twenty to twenty-five years, the KJV is the second most purchased translation of the Bible. The other way in which the KJV survives is in the versions, the translations that have been made deliberately modifying what went before. So if you read from the New Revised Version or the American Standard Version, you are still getting an awful lot of the King James Bible."

—Mark Noll
Professor of History; University of Notre Dame, Indiana

letters, either directly or differently inspired by the KJV. In the mid-1850s, both Nathaniel Hawthorne and Herman Melville wrote biblically instigated novels, with Hawthorne inspiring his newfound friend Melville to turn his early whaling saga *Moby Dick* into a Leviathan epic. The King James Bible permeates Melville's narrative from its opening words ("Call me Ishmael") through Father Maple's crow's-nest-pulpit sermon, up from the book of Jonah, to Captain Ahab's very name and his ultimate drowning and climaxing damnation.

Immensely key to the fateful coming of secession and Civil War was the 1851 appearance of Harriet Beecher Stowe's *Uncle Tom's Cabin*, a household sentimental novel that "swept the nation like a cyclone." Indeed, it swept the entire world before Lincoln's election in 1860. As Lincoln himself said on meeting her, "So this is the little lady who started this great big war." Awkwardly tragic in its escapist plot, it still stood alone in confronting the issue of slavery, "the monstrous actuality that existed under the very noses of its readers," writes Kenneth Lynn. "Mrs. Stowe roused emotions . . . in order to facilitate the moral regeneration of the entire nation. Mrs. Stowe was deeply serious—a sentimentalist with a vengeance" exercised right out of the KJV. Her main slave character

cannot write, but Tom has a Bible, and he reads slowly, laboring over each salvational word.

"Let—not—your—heart—be—troubled. In—my—Father's—house—are—many—mansions. I—go—to—prepare—a—place—for—you."

After the Civil War came the bread-and-circuses bestseller *Ben Hur*, the Roman charioteer/convert whom the Union general Lew Wallace immortalized midst Christian persecution. His subtitle was *A Tale of the Christ*, who doesn't show up for the first hundred pages. But Wallace did set the gaudy parameters for Hollywood's forays into the Bible as mass entertainment drawing from either Testament, all the star-studded way to Richard Burton striking the sacred rent in the fabric of *The Robe*.

More modern American fiction clings penitentially to the words of the KJV when William Faulkner reaches all the way back to Tyndale for the story and title of one of his greatest evocations, *Absalom, Absalom*, or couches *The Sound and the Fury* as a Christian allegory, right down to the salvational preaching at a Black church meeting. Even Ernest Hemingway turns to Ecclesiastes for *The Sun Also Rises*, and his succinct, classic short story, "A Clean, Well-Lighted Place," recites the Lord's Prayer from the KJV to the sobering nihilism of "Our nada who art in nada, nada be thy nada. . . ."

But from others more believing in the Word, there are the cautionary tales of Flannery O'Connor—or Marilynne Robinson's novels, brilliantly immersed in religious life out in mid-Western churches without a snarling thump upon any Bible. *Gilead* won Robinson a Pulitzer Prize for her deeply biblical probing through three generations of preachers in search of what balm might yet be found in Gilead, Ohio—and not an Elmer Gantry among them.

Such cultural forces surely reinforce faith and credence in the KJV—for both its religious message and intellectual majesty intertwined. Yet it is difficult to gauge any abiding depth in present-day religious commitment

St. Peter Denying Christ by Gustave Doré, *The Doré Bible Illutrations*, Dover Publications.

except among voting evangelists. Perhaps the strongest pressures do not come not from the disappearance of strict beliefs. The centrifugal dispersion may arise more from a general indifference, the public lack of interest in any information other than the running script of the Internet, text messages, Twittering, or image blasts and overworked debate over television. The Gallup poll finds that 93 percent of Americans believe in a living God. Many claim somehow to be church-affiliated. But does that bring people together in any expenditure of quality time in worship or move the congregations in today's mega-churches beyond "the bells and whistles" of banal optimism? Who would attend to God's Word on their only Sunday off unless it makes them feel good?

Many see an overall advantage in using contemporaneous ways and means to spread the "good news." But sometimes it pays to look more closely at just how breezily certain emotionally tense passages of holy writ are being easily rephrased. Once again, Daniell brings us back to the Garden of Gethsemane and that fateful night when Peter kept meeting with what are too readily called "challenges," three altogether, before the cock crowed at dawn. Daniell recalls the passage—raised musically to spiritual heights by J. S. Bach's *St. Matthew's Passion*—that settles "down the ages" at the end of Matthew 26 by Tyndale, as carried over to the KJV:

> And Peter remembered the words of Jesus which said unto him: before the cock crow, thou shalt deny me thrice: and he went out of the doors and wept bitterly. (Matt. 26:75)

Daniell precisely points to the Greek *pikros* for "sharply," "harshly," or "bitterly" and how rhythmically it sweeps out of "wept," whether spoken or sung. Then he ponders how the Contemporary English Version (1995) "welcomes" its readers on page vi with these assurances:

> The *Contemporary English Version* has been described as "a user-friendly" and "mission-driven" translation that can be *read aloud* without stumbling, *heard* without misunderstanding, and *listened to* with enjoyment and appreciation, because the style is lucid and lyrical.

All well and good, but on this cheery promise, how does the CEV translate that last sentence of Peter's passion full of shock and humiliation? "Then Peter went out and cried hard."

The impact of "cried hard" is not only empty and lacking sense, it is ugly. Daniell protests that "crying hard" is what babies do for a bottle—a plea lacking any serious awareness of betrayal, disloyalty, guilt, sorrow, or other emotions Peter was likely to experience. But the words are also clunky. How could any Bach have possibly set those two clenched monosyllables to any tragic strain of music? Similar clunkers occur throughout the CEV and elsewhere in equivalently translated pieces of writing. What they are missing is the aesthetic richness of so many passages in the KJV, the aura and emotional depths and majesty of belief expressed in its inherited English prose.

Can anything be salvaged from this shameless effrontery to past biblical grandeur, originally born of a revered common English? How can we halt and perhaps reverse this trashing of the Good Book—once created as a Great Read, now being dumbed down into an easy and ever easier "Take"?

So speculates book collector Donald E. Brake amidst his many shelves of rare English Bibles. Brake finds that two extreme opinions are widely held. Some believe the KJV is the only version truly inspired by God, period. But too many others dismiss the KJV as an old-fashioned version unable to speak with any reliable or comprehensible effect to the modern Christian community.

The first is like the Texan who is rumored to have said, upon rejecting a new translation, "If the English of the Saint James Bible was good enough for Jesus, it's good enough for me." There indeed exist "KJV Only" enclaves who declaim that the KJV was written in eternity, and that Abraham and Moses and the prophets all read the 1611 KJV, including the New

Continuing Value of King James Bible

"The King James remains a Bible worth reading in part because it is slightly difficult, and therefore makes you work at what you read. I think this is very useful. The Bible wasn't necessarily meant to be easy. Why otherwise would we have thousands of years of commentary on the Bible elucidating it? It is worth remembering that the Bible requires real concentrated attention, and if you have got one that is just slightly difficult to read, that actually is helpful. The Bible isn't to be dumbed down.

"Then the King James Version is, I also think, a superb translation in its sensitivity to the language of the originals in being a primarily literal translation. The KJV trusted what was in the originals rather than converting all that into paraphrase. So it gives one a very close sense of what the Hebrew and the Greek are saying. And as a result, in lots of places, it has produced wonderful phrases, really beautiful English that helps produce a feeling of religious awe, if you like. And religion isn't just the meaning of the words in the Bible, though that is a huge part of it. It is also a feeling in the heart, very much an emotional thing. And the language of the Kings James Bible, more than any other English Bible, can bring forth that emotion."

—David Norton

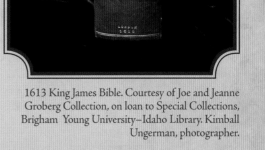

1613 King James Bible. Courtesy of Joe and Jeanne Groberg Collection, on loan to Special Collections, Brigham Young University–Idaho Library. Kimball Ungerman, photographer.

Testament. These individuals believe the Hebrew is actually English. . . . Such groups are, for obvious reasons, very small.

But the other folks make a like mistake in a quite different way, because they are freebooting on the idea that the Bible has always been some revision of another version that was revised from a previous version of the envisioned Word of God. So that it makes no never mind if another rendering jives these ancient stories into the jargon and

"As a by-product of checking the translation orally, working toward the greatest accuracy possible, the Bible does arrive at eloquence. But that is not the goal, not the purpose. It is not important as a literary artifact. It is important because it is to be a repository of religious truth. And yes, it is nice that religious truth is couched in eloquence, but that is not the first goal."

—Susannah Monta
Professor of English; University of Notre Dame, Indiana

language of the moment, within the limited vocabulary of present-day usage, from an altogether ahistorical point of view that asks nothing interpretive from any human mind. Only the mental comfort of the reader counts, no matter how meager the dumbing-down leaves behind any true Biblical meaning.

Against such trends, the KJV has become the last preserve of an historic moment when the English language was in its golden age and the Christian faith stood, passionately—if often tragically—upon its highest mount of modern temporal expression. In the sixteenth and seventeenth centuries, everybody still lived in later biblical times. Language was the primary gift and indelible mark of an educated man—or woman, lest we forget Good Queen Bess as one inspiration of that golden age, hers. And the gift and use of the English language was how many a believer

Lilies of the Field

The lilies of the field—such a beautiful phrase. I've heard translations, contemporary translations, for example, that have switched that out for "wildflowers." Is "wildflowers" more accurate? I don't know. Maybe it does convey in some sense some more accurate picture. But, the liturgical value of the phrase "lilies of the field," it's alliterative. You have "lilies" and then the "l" comes back in field. It's such a beautiful—the person who thought of that phrasing was convinced of the preciousness of this revelation and wanted to make sure that that beauty was available. That's what I mean by, in a sense, his soul is in the translation—"The lilies of the field."

—John C. Cavadini
Theologian; University of Notre Dame, Indiana

> 24 Confider the rauens: for they neith fowe nor reape, which neither haue ſtorehouſe nor barne, and *yet* God feedeth them: how much more are ye better then foules?
>
> 25 And which of you with taking thought can adde to his ſtature one cubite?
>
> 26 If yee then bee not able to doe the leaſt thing, why take ye thought for the remnant?
>
> 27 Confider the lilies how they grow: they labour not, neither ſpin they: yet I ſay vnto you, that Salomon himſelfe in all his royaltie was not clothed like one of theſe.
>
> 28 If then God ſo clothe the graſſe wh

Courtesy of Harold B. Lee Special Collections; BYU Library. Kimball Ungerman, photographer.

displayed the furthest reach of his or her civilized intelligence in order to speak the received truth of their soaring hearts.

Admittedly, the KJV can sometimes be trying to read, as it adheres so closely to a literal translation.

But there is often an exceptional beauty in its simplest phrase.

And those lilies of the valley (field) marched right on to "In the beauty of the lilies, Christ was born across the sea/With a glory in his bosom that transfigures you and me:/As he died to make men holy, let us die to make men free" . . . from yet another Victorian lady, the stalwart Julia Ward Howe, who wrote the *Battle Hymn of the Republic*. The KJV's undeniable eloquence then passed to John Updike as one of his most provocative titles, *In the Beauty of the Lilies*, full of moral import from the early days of World War I to those at the fatal compound of David Koresh. In fact, Updike's fine novel is a religious tracking (not a tract) of American beliefs across the harrowed twentieth century through loss of faith, rise of social freedoms, survival of local virtues, and even the

"I wouldn't want to talk about the King James Bible, as such. It is almost an accident that it became the English Bible, that for two and a half centuries, it was almost the only English Bible in common use. What I would want to talk about is the influence of the Tyndale tradition—of that set of Biblical translations from Tyndale's own through the Great Bible. The Geneva Bible, the Bishops' Bible that finished with the Authorized Version, the King James translation that builds on all that have come before it."

—Alec Ryrie

Professor of the History of Christianity; Durham University, England

evil rise of satanic cults. Yet it desperately keeps eloquent hold of lasting mores, if not biblical truth.

And that first goal was deeply moral. As one churchman has observed, "There is no other teaching that has brought about as much protection for the dignity and freedom of humankind."

Consider only one line from Milton's *Paradise Lost*. Again, in Genesis, we are back in the Garden of Eden with Eve having returned from eating the fruit of the tree of knowledge of good and evil. Both Adam and Eve are trying to hide in shame from their God. He finds them out and confronts Adam, who confesses: "She gave me of the tree and I did eat." A precise line of simple, one-syllable words, it is also a perfect iambic pentameter. It is exactly what Adam would guiltily confess, but it is also straight out of the King James Version—which was Milton's own contemporary Bible (when he too wasn't consulting the Geneva). This incomparable line, quoted from

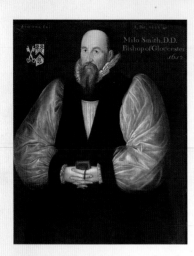

Miles Smith, 1616, helped translate the King James Version of the Bible. Courtesy Wikimedia Commons.

even earlier sources, had everlasting effect on Milton's epic poem, one of the great treasures of English literature.

Here the biblical text is caught in the very act of evolving into living Christian culture. That spiritual inherence within the KJV was recognized by one of its most talented—if establishmentarian—revisers, Bishop of Gloucester Miles Smith, who served as the final editor and wrote the Bible's preface, "The Translators to the Readers." His several pages are recommended reading for two reasons. First, they provide a lively first draft of the history that informed the long struggle to create an English Bible up through the KJV. And second, his words recognize the potential of the KJV to accommodate future interpretations of holy scripture, arguing that in setting forth God's Word, "fearefulness would better beseeme vs then confidence."

Miles Smith is also one of those bishops who preferred to quote from the Geneva Version in his own sermons. (He even quoted from the Geneva in his preface.) His preface argues for the likelihood of alterations to the Bible at the margins—literally, in the very margins of these King James Bible pages, reserved for limited notes—and he speaks forthrightly about how the translators have controlled their proffered text.

> Lastly, wee haue on the one side auoided the scrupulosity of the Puritanes, who leaue the olde Ecclesiasticall words, and betake them to other, as when they put *washing* for *Baptisme*, and *Congregation* in stead of *Church* : as also on the other side we haue shunned the obscuritie of the Papists, in their *Azimes Tunike, Rational, Holocausts, Proepuce, Pasche,* and a number of such like, whereof their late Translation [the Rheims] is full, and that of purpose to darken the sence, that since they must needs translate the Bible, yet by the language thereof, it may be kept from being understood. But we desire that the Scripture may speak like it selfe, as in the language of *Canaan*, that it may bee understood euen of the very vulgar.

Bishop Smith declares that "if we will resolue, to resolue vpon modestie with *S. Augustine*, it is better to make doubt about those things which are secret, then to striue about those things that are uncertaine."

As the KJV gradually evolved into the Authorized Version, it did so across *all* the Judeo-Christian spectrums of belief. It did not do so out of any sectarian or proselytizing agendas, but by a visionary process of seeking to transpose and give voice to the perceivable Word of God. It kept telling the stories of the Old and New Testaments in indomitable words that echoed through the open chambers of the world—cathedrals, churches, synagogues, cloisters, chapels, halls for oratorio, camp meetings, tabernacles, revival tents—wherever any two are gathered together in the name of the Lord. Let us continue to search the numerous foundations of modern

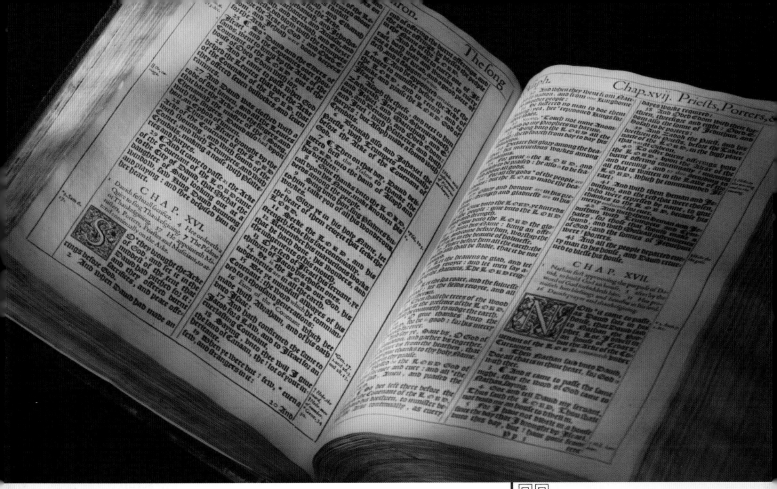

belief—always with an eye to catching some glimpse of the influence of God Himself . . . but let us know that we will never have another Bible that so powerfully expresses God's inerrant and perfect love.

An original King James Bible.
Courtesy of FIRES OF FAITH;
Groberg Films and BYU Broadcasting;
Harold B. Lee Special Collections,
BYU Library.

"The King James Bible has had an amazing tenacity. It has hung on in the affection of particular churches and of whole peoples in a way that a 400-year-old text really shouldn't. I think the King James translators themselves would be amazed that a 400-year-old translation is still being used. "But the Bible is an essential for Christians. We absolutely need it. It is the means by which we can hear God speaking to us. But a day will come when we will meet him face to face and then we can leave our Bibles at home."

—Alec Ryrie
Professor of the History of Christianity; Durham University, England

REFERENCES

Chapter One

Page 1   In 1603, two kingdoms—Donald L. Brake, *A Visual History of the English Bible* (Grand Rapids, Michigan: Baker Books, 2008), 184–185

Page 1   "this sceptered isle"—William Shakespeare, *Richard the Second*, II:1, John of Gaunt, lines 40–46

Page 1   "Who but our cousin in Scotland?"—Benson Broderick, *Wide as the Waters* (New York: Simon & Schuster, 2001), 199.

Page 2   Mary, Queen of Scots and Almost of England (sidebar)—Brake, 177. See also Antonia Fraser, *Mary Queen of Scots* (New York: Delacorte, 1969).

Page 2   "If I swear on the book" (sidebar)—Fraser, 531–532.

Page 2   Over the ensuing years, the party who bore (sidebar)—Pauline Croft, *King James* (Basingstoke and New York: Palgrave Macmillan, 2003).

Page 3   had himself done metrical translations of thirty psalms—David Daniell, *The Bible in English* (New Haven and London: Yale University Press, 2003), 428.

Page 3   He also had a godly fear of witchcraft—Croft, 261.

Page 3   Shakespeare was aware of this royal interest in sorcery—John Keay and Julia Keay, *Collins Encyclopedia of Scotland* (London: HarperCollins, 1994), 556; David Harris Willson, *King James VI & I* (London: Longman: 1963), 103–105.

Page 4   shall change the Church of England—Brake, 183.

Page 4   At the very close of the conference—Brake, 183; Daniell, 432–433.

Page 4   "May your Majesty be pleased"—Ibid.

Page 4   If every man's humour should be followed—Brake, 183–184; Daniell, 433.

Page 5   "Whereupon his Highness wished that some special pains"—Daniell, 433.

Page 5   "(professing that he could never yet see a Bible well translated in English"—Daniell, 433; Brake, 184.

Page 5   "given him by an English lady"—Daniell, 433.

Page 6   "the richt excellent richt high and michtie price James the Sext . . . the first Bible printed in Scotland"—Ibid.

Page 6   "yet hereupon did his Majesty begin to bethink"—Daniell, 435; see also Daniell, "The Translators to the Reader," 786.

Chapter Two

Page 8   Yet again, there remains the uncertain provenance of even these hallowed documents—Brake, 25.

Page 8   The earliest extant scrap of any Old Testament dates from the Babylonian captivity in 586 b.c.—Brake, 25–26.

Page 8   Jewish revolts against the Assyrians (168 b.c.) and finally the Romans (135 a.d.)—Brake, 26.

Page 8   The Dead Sea Scrolls date from the century before Christ's birth to the century after His ministry on earth—Brake, 28.

Page 9   In 112 a.d., Pliny described how the medium was produced—Pliny, *Natural History*, bk. 33, par. 20–24.

Page 9   The Greek word for "books" is *biblia*—hence, *Bible*—Brake, 29.

Page 9   The great library in Alexandria, Egypt—Brake, 29–30.

Page 11   These were called "miniatures"—Bruce R. Metzger, *Manuscripts of the Greek Bible: An Introduction to Greek Palaeography* (New York: Oxford University Press, 1981), 45.

Page 11   Then one dedicated scholar—Eusebius Hieronymus—came forth—Brake, 31–32.

Page 11   St. Jerome's text became the official Latin Bible of the Roman Catholic Church, known as the Vulgate from *versio vulgata*, "the published version"—H. D. F. Sparks, "Jerome as Biblical Scholar," in *The Cambridge History of the Bible*, vol. 1, *From the Beginnings to Jerome*, ed. P. R. Ackroyd and C. F. Evans (Cambridge: Cambridge University Press, 1970), 519.

Page 11   "once for all delivered version"—Ibid.

Page 11   "Billfrith, the anchorite, who forged the ornaments"—Robert G. Calkins, *Illuminated Books of the Middle Ages* (Ithaca, NY: Cornell University Press, 1970), 63.

Page 12   *Syllic waes se sigebeam*—"The Dream of the Rood," quoted in Daniell, 51.

Page 12   Not until the fourteenth century did a righteous dissenter arise—Brake, 48–49; Bodleian Library, *Wycliffe and His Followers* (Oxford: Bodleian Library, 1983), 9.

Page 13   "It seems first that knowledge of God's law should be taught in that tongue that is more known"—"Lollardy," *Dictionary of the Christian Church*, ed. F. L. Cross (London: Oxford University Press, 1929), 19.

Page 14   "Do you have a Bible in English, or have you memorized any portion of an English translation?"—Brake, 66.

Page 14   posthumous vengeance upon Wycliffe—Brake, 266–267.

Pages 14–15   The Avon to the Severn runs—Unknown poet, quoted in *Wide as the River Is*, 73.

Page 15   In truth, the Word was being far more commonly dramatized outside the church—on the play wagons in the medieval town squares—Daniell, 102–104.

Page 15 A bird have I brought/To my bairn—A. C. Cawley, ed., *The Wakefield Pageants of the Towneley Cycle* (Manchester, 1958), 62: *Secunda Pasorum*, lines 722–727 (modernized).

Chapter Three

Page 16 Luther's intense studies of *sola Christus* ("Christ alone")—Brake, 86.

Page 16 Young Martin Luther, born the son of a copper miner, was meant to be a lawyer, but a thunderstorm scared him into becoming a monk—Brake, 84–88.

Page 17 On October 31, 1517, Luther posted his ninety-five articles—Brake, 89.

Page 18 Luther was taken by friends into hiding as "Knight George"— Brake, 83.

Page 18 "Those Heretics who pretend that the laity need not know God's law"—R. L. P. Milburn, "The 'People's Bible': Artists and Commentators," in *The Cambridge History of the Bible*, vol. 2, *The West from the Fathers to the Reformation*, ed. G. W. H. Lampe (Cambridge: Cambridge University Press, 1969), 292–293.

Page 18 Printing in the West had actually begun around 1450 in Germany at Mainz, with experiments in "artificial writing" by a goldsmith named Johann Gutenberg—Brake, "The Man Behind the Book," 70–73.

Page 20 He was never an idler or spendthrift—G. S. Wegener, *6000 Years of the Bible* (London: Hodder and Stoughton, 1985), 192.

Page 20 "unbridled whims"—Wegener, 193.

Page 20 Fust took over the press, shop, and Bibles and made himself and his family a tidy fortune—Don Cleveland Norman, *The 500th Pictorial Census of the Gutenberg Bible* (Chicago: Coverdale Press, 1961), 11.

Page 20 But later scholarship, via x-ray examination of one leaf from the Bible, suggests that Gutenberg was only trying to protect his business secrets—Ruth Pritchard, "Roll Over Gutenberg," *Alaskan Airlines Magazine* (February 1987), 32–33. "Dr. Pritchard goes into great detail," comments Brake, "in describing the scientific experiment by Tom Cahill and Dick Schwab included in the following account."

Page 21 Guilliame Fichet, revived his reputation—Brake, 73.

Page 21 Despite such dangers, these *incunabula* were flooding the market—Norman, 14.

Page 21 Among these freely printed books, Luther's German Bible flourished—Brake, 89–90.

Page 21 "Unless I am convinced by the testimony of the scriptures"—Graham Tomlin, *Luther and His World* (Downers Grove, IL: InterVarsity, 2002), 109.

Chapter Four

Page 24 William Tyndale, likely born in 1494, was a Gloucestershire man—Daniell, 140–141.

Page 24 proved himself remarkably fluent in eight languages—Daniell, 142; J. F. Mozley, *William Tyndale* (London: SPCK, 1937), 65.

Page 24 while serving as tutor to the children of the powerful Lady Anne Poyntz Walsh of Little Sodbury Manor—Daniell, 141.

Pages 24–25 a Catholic priest who cynically unburdened himself "that we're better without God's law," that he much preferred "the pope's law"—Daniell, 142.

Page 25 "Maister Tyndall hearing that, answered him"—Daniell, 142; John Foxe, *The Acts and Monuments of John Foxe* (1563), 514; Foxe, 1877, IV, 117.

Page 25 "the word of God is quick [alive] . . ."—Daniell, 266; William Tyndale, trans., *Tyndale's New Testament* (New Haven, CT: Yale University, 1989), 350.

Page 26 The Greek was *koiné*—the common, spoken tongue of the Eastern empire—Daniell, 133.

Page 27 "the properties of the Hebrew tongue"—Daniell, 234; William Tyndale, *The Obediance of a Christian Man* (Antwerp, 1528), ed. with introduction by David Daniell (2000), 19. "The properties of the Hebrew tongue agreeth a thousand times more with the English than with the Latin. The manner of speaking is both one; so that in an thousand places thou needst not but translate it into the English word for word when thou must seek a compass [go around] in the Latin [. . .] so that it have the same grace and sweetness, sense and pure understanding with it in the Latin, as it hath in the Hebrew."

Page 27 Second, Tyndale also wrote at the peak of the highest, most lively development of the English language that was newly coming into fruition—Daniell, 136–137.

Page 27 the Christmas story of the shepherds come from their flocks by night to worship the Christ child—Daniell, 139.

Page 28 Third . . ., Tyndale had the complete author's mastery over the rhetoric of his biblical text—Daniell, 137.

Page 29 And so was Tyndale charged by Sir Thomas More, Lord Chancellor—Daniell, 149.

Page 29 "discharging a filthy foam of blasphemies out of his brutish beastly mouth"—Daniell, 149; *Complete Works of St. Thomas More*, VIII, iii, 1260.

Page 29 his first recorded business was in Cologne with Peter Quentell to print sheets of his New Testament up through Matthew 22—Daniell, 143–144.

Page 30 By 1526, a small printer in Worms—son of the "Gutenberg" Peter Schoeffer—had printed Tyndale's New Testament in smaller octavo size—Daniell, 144–146.

Page 30–31 "in the english tongue that pestiferous and moste pernicious poison dispersed throughout all our dioces of London in great number"—Daniell, 144; Alfred W. Pollard, ed., *Records of the English Bible 1525–1611* (Oxford, 1911), 134.

Page 31 burned "many hundreth, both heir and beyond the see"—Ibid., 125

Page 31 Today, we have only one remaining complete copy of Tyndale's 1526 New Testament—Brake, 101; Daniell, 145–146.

Page 31 "Let it not make thee despair neither yet discourage thee O reader"—Daniell, 147; Tyndale, *Obedience*, 2000, 3.

Page 31 "Hans Luft of Marlborow" brought out both *Mammon* and *Obedience*—Daniell, 146.

Page 32 Tyndale was living under the protection of Thomas Poyntz at the English House in Antwerp, where a dissenting minister named John Rogers arrived to serve as chaplain to resident English merchants in 1534—Daniell, 153.

Page 32 "we may apply the medicine of the scripture, every man to his own sores"—Daniell, 148; *Tyndale's Old Testament*, 7.

Page 34 One copy of this New Testament belonged to Queen Anne Boleyn herself—Daniell, 147.

Page 34 The agreed estimate of the debt in words owed William Tyndale by those who "translated" the New Testament in the King James Version is 83 percent—Daniell, 152. "The true figure is 83 percent," insists Daniell in Chapter Nine, note 13. "See John Neilson and Royal Skousen, 'How Much of the King James Bible is William Tyndale's?' *Reformation*, III (1998), 49–74. Note the refutation there of Butterworth's figure of 18 percent (in his *Literary Lineage of the King James Bible*, 1941) from a double methodological error."

Chapter Five

Page 35 "the great danger wherewith I am everywhere encompassed"—Daniell, 153; also David Daniell, *William Tyndale: A Biography* (New Haven and London, 1994), 213.

Page 36 "for his learning and judgment in scripture, he is more worthy to be promoted than all the bishops in England"—Daniell, *The Bible in English*, 152; Foxe, 1877, v, 130–134.

Page 36 An uncertain Tyndale was willing to speak of his misery as early as 1531 to Stephen Vaughan, who was Henry VIII's factor in the Netherlands—Daniell, *The Bible in English*, 150–151.

Page 36 "I assure you, if it would stand with the king's most gracious pleasure to grant only a bare text of the scripture"—*Fires of Faith* Script, 42, based on Stephen Vaughan's letter to Cromwell after his April 1531 meeting with Tyndale in Antwerp; Daniell, *The Bible in English*, 151.

Page 37 But Tyndale's entrapment still required a Judas . . . —Henry Phillips, a transient, debauched young Englishman who insinuated himself into Tyndale's trusting company—Daniell, *The Bible in English*, 153–154.

Page 37 "that they pitied to see his simplicity when they took him"—Daniell, *The Bible in English*, 153; Foxe, 1877, v, 128.

Page 37 "The king's grace," Poyntz pressed forward, "should have of him [Tyndale] at this day as high a treasure as any man living"—Daniell, *William Tyndale: A Biography*, 370.

Page 38 The flight of Phillips did not stop Tyndale's trial from inexorably proceeding before seventeen commissioners, led by three chief accusers, under the greatest grand inquisitor in Europe, Jacobus Latomus—Daniell, *The Bible in English*, 154–156.

Page 38 his "last, lost" book in detail—Robert J. Wilkinson, "Reconstructing Tyndale in Latomus: William Tyndale's Last, Lost Book," *Reformation*, I (1966), 252–285, 345–400.

Page 40 In August 1536, William Tyndale was condemned as a heretic—Daniell, *The Bible in English*, 156–157.

Page 40 "Lord, open the king of England's eyes!"—Foxe, 1877, v, 127; Hall, 1548, reprinted 1809, 818.

Page 40 "At the town's end is a notable solemn place of execution, where worthy William Tyndale was unworthily put to death"—Daniell, *William Tyndale: A Biography*, 384.

Chapter Six

Page 41 Miles Coverdale—a milder English colleague in Antwerp—brought out the first complete English Bible—Brake, 111–112.

Page 41 "Sure I am," Coverdale professes, "that there cometh more knowledge"—Brake, 111, quoting from Miles Coverdale, *Dedications and Prologues to the Translation of the Bible* (1535; repr., Cambridge: Cambridge University Press, 1846), 19.

Page 42 John Hooker of Exeter (sidebar)—Brake, 112, quoted in J. F. Mozley, *Coverdale and His Bibles* (Cambridge: Lutterworth Press, 1953), reprint 2005, 16.

Page 42 under the mastership of his new prior, Robert Barnes, and dedicated himself "wholly unto Christ," but "with a friendly and upright nature and very gentle spirit"—Daniell, *The Bible in English*, 176–177; Bale, 1548, 721; Mozley, 3.

Page 42 "a vehement wind, overturning mountains and rocks"—Ibid.

Page 42 Depending on "five sundry interpreters" to help him, he wrote *Unto the Christian Reader* in 1535—Daniell, *The Bible in English*, 176 passim.

Page 42 "quaint"—Daniell, *The Bible in English*, 183; "In Jeremiah 8:22, in KJV the haunting question 'Is there no balm in Gilead?' is in Coverdale the statement 'For there is no Treacle at Gilead.'"

Page 42 C. S. Lewis called him "a rowing-boat among battleships"— C. S. Lewis, *The Literary Impact of the Authorized Version* (London: The Athlone Press, 1950), 11 passim.

Page 43 Out of his admiration for the German multiple-compounding interpreters, Coverdale also liked to coin and straddle compound neologisms in English—Daniell, *The Bible in English*, 181.

Page 43 Coverdale honored Tyndale's crucial choices of Christ's Word in support of Pauline doctrine, such as *congregation*, *elder*, and, above all, *love*—Daniell, *The Bible in English*, 181 passim.

Page 43   mildly alter the seventh commandment to read, "Thou shalt not break wedlock"—Brake, 119; for more detailed coverage of Coverdale's text, see Mozley, *Coverdale and His Bibles*, 78–109.

Page 43   his genuine triumph came in his sweetly and smoothly flowing translations of the Latin Psalms—Daniell, *The Bible in English*, 181.

Page 43   David Daniell makes an historical point: "The Church of England at worship sang or said Coverdale every day for over four hundred years"—Ibid.

Page 44   Finally, Coverdale's Bible was the first to separate out the fourteen (or fifteen) "hidden" books between the Old and New Testaments—Daniell, *The Bible in English*, 186–188.

Page 44   "These books (good reader) which are called Apocrypha"—DHM (Darlow, Moule, and Herbert), 187–188.

Page 45   "as a public means of validating Henry's claim to govern without clerical intercession as the sole intermediary between temporal society and the divine order"—John H. King, "Henry VIII as David: The King's Image and Reformation Politics," in *Rethinking the Henrician Era: Essays on Early Tudor Texts and Contexts*, Peter C. Herman, ed. (Urbana, IL: University of Illinois Press, 1994), 78.

Page 45   "as yet they had no leisure"—SP (*State Papers Domestic . . . Henry VIII*), 1830, I, 592.

Page 45   Who saved that cache of Tyndale manuscripts—Daniell, *The Bible in English*, 191–192.

Page 46   John Rogers emerges from this venture as another of those reforming church dignitaries who valiantly risked exile abroad—Daniell, *The Bible in English*, 191–195.

Page 46   "a learned man . . . with a noble character"—Mozley, 1993, 122–123.

Page 47   Rogers bravely guided "Matthew's Bible"—Daniell, *The Bible in English*, 193–195.

Page 47   "To the most noble and gracious Prince King Henry the eight"—as well as to obtain a royal license for this English version of the Bible. Right on the title page, it said, "Set forth with the King's most gracious license"—Daniell, *The Bible in English*, 194.

Page 47   The Bible was promptly popular . . . Cranmer—now archbishop himself—wrote Cromwell, "So far as I have read thereof I like it better than any other translation heretofore made"—SP, 1830, I, 561–562; Pollard, 1911, 215.

Page 47   Cromwell wished for even more copies, fully nine thousand to cover all the parishes in England, and he encouraged daily readings through action by the justices of the peace to set local watch over recalcitrant parish priests—Daniell, *The Bible in English*, 195; A. G. Dickens, *The English Reformation* (2/1989), 115.

Page 48   only visible reference to William Tyndale in Matthew's Bible—Ibid.

Page 48   one other distinctive feature to Matthew's Bible—its own unique frontispiece—Daniell, *The Bible in English*, 196.

Page 48   life didn't turn out that way for John Rogers, the maker of Matthew's Bible—Daniell, *The Bible in English*, 191-192, *passim*.

Page 50   "he, as one feeling no smart, washed his hands in the flame, as though it had been in cold water"—Foxe, 1877, VL, 611–612.

Chapter Seven

Page 51   It came to be called the Great Bible, which it surely was by virtue of its sharply increased page size—Daniell, *The Bible in English*, 204–205.

Page 52   The editing and revisions of the Great Bible were assigned to Miles Coverdale, a politic choice—L&P (*Letters and Papers . . . Henry III*) XII, ii, 841–842, 171.

Page 53   "Not only the same bibles being XXV in number were seized and made confiscate, but also the printer, merchants and correctors with great jeopardy of their lives escaped"—Daniell, *The Bible in English*, 201. Quoted in S. L. Greenslade, ed., *The Coverdale Bible*, 1935, (1975), 151; and Slavin, 1979, 12; in a prior note, Daniel, *passim* : "I am indebted in these pages to Professor A. J. Slavin; not only for his 'The Rochepot Affair' *Sixteenth Century Journal*, X (1979), pp. 3–19 . . . but for further details of his from his unpublished paper, 'Tyndale's Revenge: Henry VIII Gives an English Bible to the People', given at the Tyndale Symposium, The Huntington Library, October 1996, and for private communication."

Page 53   "Cromwell met with Castillon [the French ambassador in London]"—Daniell, *The Bible in English*, 202; Slavin, 1979, 12, n. 4.

Page 53   But the newly acclaimed earl was already beginning to lose his grip on power at the hands of the vengeful Duke of Norfolk—Daniell, *The Bible in English*, 203.

Page 54   Tyndale had been especially outspoken in favor of married clergy—Daniell, *The Bible in English*, 226.

Page 54   "He must have a wife for two causes"—Tyndale, *Obedience*, 2000, 86–87.

Page 54   On June 10, 1540—only weeks after the Great Bibles first reached their churches—Cromwell was arrested at the Council Table for heresy and treason—Daniell, *The Bible in English*, 204.

Page 54   The surrounding illustrations on that same title page, however, thoroughly depict what remained the true state of affairs across all of England—Daniell, *The Bible in English*, 205–207.

Page 55   quelled dissenters are already behind bars—Daniell, throughout, notes: "A good account of the title-page, and the impact of the Great Bible, is given by David Scott Kastan, 'The Noise of the New Bible': Reform and Reaction in Henrician England," in *Religion and Culture in Renaissance England*, ed. Claire McEachern and Debra Shuger (Cambridge, 1997)," 46–68.

Page 56   After Cromwell's execution in 1540, his coat-of-arms was removed from the title page of the fourth edition, not unlike the name of a condemned Soviet member of the Politburo being removed from atop Lenin's tomb—Daniell, *The Bible in English*, 208.

Page 56   In contrast, the reaction of the English commoners to these handsome English Bibles was ecstatic, then increasingly disorderly—Brake, 139–140.

Page 56   "without disputation"—Brake, 139.

Page 56   then the sharp threat of persecution. Hugh Latimer—Daniell, *The Bible in English*, 338.

Page 56   *On the Plough* that compared plowing to preaching, the labor and duty of all bishops: "scripture calleth it meat; not strawberries, that come but once a year, and tarry not long, but are soon gone"—Ibid. "Six of Latimer's sermons are reprinted in *Hugh Latimer: The Sermons* (Manchester, 2000); see also page 35: this famous remark is in *Latimer*, ed. G. E. Corne, 1844, I, 2.

Page 57   "Be of good cheer, master Riley"—Foxe, 1877, VII, 550.

Page 57   At this same spot outside Balliol College, another famous martyr—the deposed Archbishop Thomas Cranmer—was burned—Daniell, *The Bible in English*, 264, with following interviews.

Page 58   first printed Pierre Robert Olivétan's French New Testament, then Olivétan's "noble folio Bible," which actually had influenced John Rogers's work in Antwerp on his Matthew's Bible—Daniell, *The Bible in English*, 196–197.

Page 59   The "learned men"—who gathered around the academy to "peruse" the existing English versions of the New Testament—Daniell, *The Bible in English*, 278.

Page 59   Consider Jesus' short parable in Luke 15:8–10—Daniell, *The Bible in English*, 284–285.

Page 60   But a crew stayed behind in Switzerland "for the space of two years and more day and night" to bring about the first English Geneva Bible in April 1560—Pollard, 1911, 280.

Page 60–61   The Geneva Version immediately became the Bible of the English people and especially of the Scots—Daniell, *The Bible in English*, 295; *Acts and Proceedings of the General Assembly of the Kirk of Scotland*, I (Edinburgh, 1840), 443.

Page 61   250 marginal notes . . . too proselytizing, but out of all of them, John Eadie neutrally finds that "not more than ten of them are unmistakably Calvinistic utterances"—John Eadie, *The English Bible*, Vol. 2 (London: MacMillan, 1876), 28.

Page 61   "the first great achievement of Elizabeth's reign"—Gerald Hammond, *The Making of the English Bible* (Manchester, 1982), 89.

Page 61   One way to glimpse the majesty of the Geneva Version is to read closely into the verses of Second Isaiah chapter 40—Daniell, *The Bible in English*, 317–318.

Page 63   that "the crooked shall be straight and the rough

places plain" along that wilderness path to Jerusalem was adroitly caught by the librettist Charles Jennens for Handel's *Messiah*, even as these very words were being taken up by the KJV—Daniell, *The Bible in English*, 574.

Page 63   exactly what Matthew Parker—newly appointed Archbishop of Canterbury by Elizabeth I in 1559—proposed—Daniell, *The Bible in English*, 338–339.

Page 64   "in jug only have the preferment of this version"—Pollard, 1911, 293–294.

Page 64   "to draw to one uniformity," she refused—Pollard, 1911, 293.

Page 64   "Words and more words is the great belief of this translator, born, no doubt, out of his belief in what constitutes good English style"—Hammond, 1982, 141.

Page 64   "In no way could it hold comparison with the Geneva Bible"—Ibid., 143.

Page 64   That the practicing Anglican clergy understood this imposition to be wrong-headed themselves is clear from a study of their continued use of the Geneva Bible in their own sermons—Daniell, *The Bible in English*, 295.

Page 64–65   reveals them taking their texts from the Geneva Bible twenty-seven times, while taking from the Bishops' Bible in only five instances—Randall T. Davidson, "The Authorization of the English Bible," *Macmillan's Magazine*, XLIV (1881), 436–444.

Page 65   Among the twenty or so remaining sermonizers, only half picked up their text from the then-recent KJV, made all the more significant since after 1616 the Geneva Bible was banned from England—Randall T. Davidson, quoted by Lloyd Eason Berry, *The Geneva Bible: A Facsimile of the 1560 Edition* (Madison, WI: University of Wisconsin Press, 1969), 19.

Page 65   "to the very end of his life Parker used his control over the Stationers' Company to prevent the Geneva version being printed in England"—Pollard, 1911, 38.

Page 65   "he did not 'trust the people' with cheap editions of the Bible, and his lack of confidence sealed the fate of the Bishops' Bible"—Ibid., 40.

Chapter Eight

Page 66   immediate task begun in 1578 was the Rheims New Testament, a translation sorely needed among English Catholics—Daniell, *The Bible in English*, 158–159, *passim*.

Page 67   "truer than the vulgar Greek itself"—From Gregory Martin's Preface.

Page 67   Cardinal Allen had been promised by Pope Sixtus V the honor of reconciling England to the papacy—J. G. Carleton, *The Part of Rheims in the Making of the English Bible* (Oxford, 1902), 13-18.

Page 67   "neither of old nor of late, ever wholly condemned all vulgar versions of Scriptures, nor have generally forbidden the faithful to read the same"—Rheims New Testament, 1582, a ii^V.

Page 68 "sing the hymns and psalms whether in known or unknown languages, as they heard them in the holy Church, though they could neither read nor know the sense, meanings and mysteries of the Same"—BL, C.110.d.2, 3–4.

Page 68 "We translate the old Latin text, not the common Greek text"—Rheims NT, 1582, b iii^r.

Page 68 "Followeth the Greek more exactly than the Protestant's translation"—Ibid.

Page 68 Ephesians 3:6, "concorporat and comparticipant," or 2 Peter 2:13, "conquinations, following on spots and delicacies," and other perplexing phrases—Sketched in B. F. Westcott, *A General View of the History of the English Bible* (1868), rev. W. A. Wright (3/1905), 245–255.

Page 68 according to Daniell's exceeding close analysis—Daniell, *The Bible in English*, 363.

Page 69 Another 80 percent of this came from Tyndale—Ibid.

Page 69 also petulant in Martin's notes to his cross-ruffing text—Daniell, *The Bible in English*, 365.

Page 69 so that William Fulke, master of Pembroke College, Cambridge, issued *A Defence*—Daniell, *The Bible in English*, 366–367; RSTC, 17503, 11430.

Page 70 given the Rheims an inadvertent extra boost up in biblical stature—Carleton, 1902, *passim*.

Page 70 A team of modern bibliophiles—T. H. Darlow, H. F. Moule, and A. S. Herbert—concludes that this round of the battle over words helped qualify the Rheims Testament for the main joust over the KJV—DMH, 104.

Page 70 "If ever a vernacular Bible was combative and tendentious [biased]—Greenslade, 1963, 162.

Chapter Nine

Page 71 "a living library and a walking study"—Brake, 186.

Page 71 "Thunder rolls round the throne"—Thomas Wyatt after his imprisonment in 1536.

Page 72 the threat of the Gunpowder Plot—Brake, 188; Geddes MacGregor, *The Bible in the Making* (London: John Murray, 1961), 111.

Page 73 William Barlow in *The Summe and Substance of the Conference*—Daniell, *The Bible in English*, 432; reproduced from Pollard, 1911, 46–47.

Page 73 "one uniforme translation . . .—Ibid.

Page 74 a really good committee—Daniell, *The Bible in English*, 436–438; as given in Pollard, 1911, 49–52.

Page 74 "and both parties of the Church were represented by some of their best men"—Pollard, 1911, 53.

Page 75 often quite worldly experience that several translators brought to their companies—Adam Nicolson, "Miracle of the King James Bible," *National Geographic*, vol. 220, no. 6 (Dec. 2011), 44.

Page 77 The translators in King James's time took an excellent way—Pollard, 1911, 61.

Page 78 fifteen rules to be observed in the translation of the Bible—Ibid., 53–55.

Page 79 "the steps which the translators followed in preparing their revision"—Ward Allen, *Translating the New Testament Epistles 1604–1611: A Manuscript from King James's Westminster Company* [Lambeth MS 98] (Nashville, Tennessee, 1977), xli–xlii.

Page 79 "But this afternoon is our translation time, and most of our company is negligent, I would have seen you"—Quoted in Allen, 1977, xii.

Page 80 That we know that members of the meeting engaged in arguments, which were sometimes violent—Ibid., xxiv.

Page 80 "the Rheims New Testament furnished to the Synoptic Gospels and Epistles in the [KJV] as many revised readings as any other version"—Ibid., xxv; see prior and following notes on Nielson and Skousen. Daniell argues that the "base remained Tyndale and Geneva, which exerted the strongest influence."

Page 80 at Romans 8:6, Paul's phrase "to be carnally minded" in the Geneva is supported—Ibid., lxv–lxvi.

Page 80 Individual translators laboured day after day over sheets from the Bishops' Bible—Ibid., lxxxiii–lxxxiv.

Page 81 Tyndale's contributions to the KJV—John Nielson and Royal Skousen, "How Much of the King James Bible is William Tyndale's?" *Reformation* III (1998), 49–74.

Chapter Ten

Page 82 the original manuscript is lost, completely disappeared—Brake, "Whatever happened to the original manuscript of the 1611 version?" 193; Daniell, *The Bible in English*, 451–460, *passim*.

Page 82 "The Bible . . . is not a book. It is a library of books"—Interview with Diarmaid MacCulloch.

Page 83 nicknamed "Avolatry," a sentimental form of worshipfulness—Daniell, *The Bible in English*, 619.

Page 83 Unhappily, the first two issues of 1611 and 1613 had mixups—Daniell, *The Bible in English*, 460. "Some two dozen 'curious editions' are listed by William J. Chamberlin, *Catalogue of Bible Translations* (Westport, Conn., 1991), 12–14"; see also Brake, "Famous Editions of the Bible," 210–211.

Page 83 "She Bibles" and "He Bibles"—Daniell, *The Bible in English*, 460.

Page 83 "Forgotten Sins" Bible (1638)—Brake, 211.

Page 83 "Unrighteous" Bible (1653)—Ibid.

Page 83 "Wicked" Bible (1631)—Brake, 191–193; Daniell, *The Bible in English*, 460; Nicolson, *National Geographic*, 45.

Page 83 For what was adjudged a skulking act—Alister E. McGrath, *In the Beginning: The Story of the King James Bible and How It Changed a Nation, a Language, and a Culture* (New York: Doubleday, 2001), 214; Daniell, *The Bible in English*, 460.

Page 84 once the Oxbridge presses became involved in this potentially lucrative publishing venture—Brake, 211–213.

Page 84 Blayney's Bible suddenly became the "Authorized Version" for the next one hundred years, using James Ussher's infamously limiting A.D. and B.C. dating of world chronology—Brake, 213.

Page 84 an over-costumed festival in a sleepy, rural backwater called Stratford-on-Avon—Daniell, *The Bible in English*, 620; Christian Deelman, *The Great Shakespeare Jubilee* (1964), 216, "for Garrick's words, in musical accompaniment, crowned by the chorus's ecstatic paean to 'The lov'd, rever'd, immortal name/Shakespeare! Shakespeare! Shakespeare!'"

Page 85 "a rich variety of styles, within one set of covers, from the Hebrew and Greek of its originals"—Daniell, *The Bible in English*, 440.

Page 85 "KJV was born archaic: it was intended as a step back"—Daniell, *The Bible in English*, 441.

Page 87 several biblical definitions of Pauline "faith"—Robert Pogue Harrison, "The Book From Which Our Literature Springs," *The New York Review of Books*, vol. LIX, no. 2, 44.

Page 87 *National Geographic* recently ran a search to find the twenty-five most oft-continuing usages—John Baxter and Amanda Hobbs, "A Bible's Gift to Language," *National Geographic*, 2011, 49–51.

Page 90 "even Puritans would grudgingly say, 'Well, it's not such a bad Church after all'"—Interview with Diarmaid MacCulloch.

Chapter Eleven

Page 91 During the nineteenth century, the KJV enjoyed huge worldwide circulation—Daniell, *The Bible in English*, 622–623, *passim*.

Page 91 reached nearly a million copies adrift eleven years after the BFBS founding in 1804—S. H. Steinberg, *Five Hundred Years of Printing*, rev. James Moran (Hamondworth, 3/1974), 278–279.

Page 91 the cataloguers Darlow, Moule, and Herbert have since found it impossible to keep count—DMH, 368.

Page 92 Occasionally, a generalizing graph appears—Daniell, *The Bible in English*, 769, *passim*.

Page 92 "What we can estimate," Daniell writes, "is the number of new translations into English, since 1526 from the original languages"—Ibid., 769.

Page 93 Work on the RV was launched in 1870 by Dr. Samuel Wilberforce, bishop of Winchester, who was not regarded as competent to undertake the task—Daniell, *The Bible in English*, 683–687.

Page 93 T. H. Huxley, the defender of evolution, said he'd rather be descended from a humble monkey than Bishop Wilberforce—For "his exact words," suggests Daniell, "as trenchant but more interesting," see Janet Browne, *Charles Darwin: The Power of Place* (2000), 122.

Page 93 David Norton argues that "the RV [Revised Version] was a compromise between the irresistible need to revise and the immovable monument" of the King James Bible—David Norton, *A History of the English Bible as Literature* (Cambridge, 2000), 331.

Page 93 "Some ancient authorities omit: 'And Jesus said, Father, forgive them; for they know not what they do'"—Brooke Foss Westcott, *Some Lessons of the Revised Version of the New Testament* (London: Hodder & Stoughton, 1897), 4.

Page 93 Still, initial sales were a runaway on both sides of the Atlantic—W. J. Heaton, *Should the Revised Version of the Scripture be Further Revised?* (Birmingham, 1905), 1–2.

Page 93 Biblical scholars still insist the RV broke the lock that the *Textus Receptus . . .* had on sound translation—F. F. Bruce, *The English Bible: A History of Translations* (1961), 141–144; detailed information on the changes can be found in Wescott, 1879, *passim*, and Joseph Barber Lightfoot, *On a Fresh Revision of the English New Testament* (London and New York: Macmillan, 1891).

Page 94 Thomas Nelson Publishers reissued the original 1611 edition packaged as a matching gift with their own modernization of the KJV in 1982—Brake, 218, *passim*

Page 94 KJV continues to comprise 15 percent of the American Bible market—Ibid., note 9.

Page 94 let us look to American culture as hinging greatly on the distribution of the KJV, from our very earliest colonial days—Brake, 249–251.

Page 95 historian Harry Stout notes that "questions of national polity and social order increasingly received the attention of the learned divines"—Harry S. Stout, "Word and Order in Colonial New England," *The Bible in America: Essays in Cultural History*, ed. Nathan O. Hatch and Mark A. Noll (New York: Oxford University Press, 1982), 25.

Page 95 the fiery preaching of Jonathan Edwards and others who encouraged unrest throughout New England—Daniell, *The Bible in English*, 551–554.

Page 95 "the corpse-cold Unitarianism of Brattle Street and Harvard College"—Ralph Waldo Emerson, quoted in Alan Heimert and Perry Miller, eds., *The Great Awakening: Documents Illustrating the Crisis and Its Consequences* (Indianapolis, IN: Bobbs-Merrill, 1967), 257.

Page 95 Young James Madison chose to stay another year at Princeton University—Interview with Mark Noll.

Page 95–96   Much legal thinking, including Chief Justice John Marshall's decisions—Ibid.

Page 96   Ben Franklin, as usual, was more skeptical of the KJV—Ibid.

Page 96   largely in Kentucky, beginning at Cane Ridge in 1801. Tens of thousands had "an outpouring of the spirit"—Sidney E. Ahlstrom, *A Religious History of the American People* (New Haven, CT: Yale University Press, 1972), 433.

Page 96   ABS promoted sixty different redactions of the KJV in what were then gigantic numbers—360,000 in 1829, a million annually by the 1860s—Margaret T. Hills, *The English Bible in America: A Bibliography of Editions of the Bible & the New Testament Published in America* (New York: American Bible Society, 1962), 37.

Page 97   "Lincoln never joined a church"—Interview with Mark Noll.

Page 99   "from traditional theological language to language as common as that used in the newspaper"—Jack Lewis, *The English Bible from KJV to NIV: A History and Evaluation* (Grand Rapids, IA: Baker, 1981), 271.

Page 100   "swept the nation like a cyclone"—Kenneth S. Lynn, introduction to Harriet Beecher Stowe, *Uncle Tom's Cabin, O, Life among the Lowly* (Cambridge, MA: Harvard University Press, 1962), ix–x.

Page 100   "the monstrous actuality that existed under the very noses of its readers"—Ibid., x.

Page 101   *Ben Hur*, the Roman charioteer/convert whom the Union general Lew Wallace immortalized midst Christian persecution—Daniell, *The Bible in English*, 731–733.

Page 102   that fateful night when Peter kept meeting with what are too readily called "challenges," three altogether, before the cock crowed at dawn—Ibid., 770–771, *passim*.

Page 103   Brake finds that two extreme opinions are widely held—Brake, 220.

Page 103–104   that the KJV was written in eternity, and that Abraham and Moses and the prophets all read the 1611 KJV, including the New Testament—James R. White, *The King James Only Controversy: Can You Trust the Modern Translations?* (Bloomington, MN: Bethany House Publishers, 1995), 6.

Page 104   the KJV has become the last preserve of an historic moment when the English language was in its golden age and the Christian faith stood, passionately—if often tragically—upon its highest mount of modern temporal expression—Brake, 222–224.

Page 105   Adam, who confesses: "She gave me of the tree and I did eat"—Book 10, *Paradise Lost*; originally from KJV, Gen. 3:12.

Page 106   Bishop of Gloucester Miles Smith, who served as the final editor and wrote the Bible's preface, "The Translators to the Readers"—Daniell, *The Bible in English*, 775–793.

Page 106   "fearefulness would better beseeme vs then confidence"—Ibid., 791.

Page 106   Lastly, wee haue on the one side auoided the scrupulosity of the Puritanes—Ibid., 792–793.

Page 106   "if we will resolue, to resolue vpon modestie with *S. Augustine*—S. Augustine, li, 8, de Genes, ad liter, Cap. 5 [Greek].